JIGSAW FAMILIES

Solving the Puzzle of Remarriage

by Michelle Cresse

Aglow Publications

A Ministry of Women's Aglow Fellowship, Int'l.
P.O. Box 1548
Lynnwood, WA 98046-1558
USA

To
Josephine Cresse,
my Naomi, a "Fancy Spice"
who loved and accepted me

Cover design by David Marty

Unless otherwise noted, all scripture quotations in this publication are from the Holy Bible, New International Version. Copyright 1973, 1978, 1984, International Bible Society. Other versions are abbreviated as follows: TLB (The Living Bible), Beck (The New Testament in the Language of Today), KJV (King James Version).

"The Brady Bunch Theme"—Copyright © 1969 Addax Music. Co., Inc. Written by Sherwood Schwartz and Frank Devol.

ISBN 0-932305-77-6

Acknowledgements

Love and support are the girders of accomplishment. This book was completed because I received a great amount of both.

Thank you—

Gordon, for the gift of time, love, and belief. Your confidence in me has lifted me higher than I could go alone.

Nichole, Gordon, and Devon, my adaptable kids.

Mom, for being available.

Charlotte Haworth, my kindred spirit who fanned the spark to life.

Dorothea Nyberg, my mentor, tireless reader, and close friend.

Carrie Ladrido, avid supporter, head cheerleader, reader, and super friend.

Carol Greenwood, an editor who cared enough to sit down with the greenest greenhorn and show her how to improve.

Gloria Chisholm, my editor, friend, and spiritual catalyst. A listener with a loving heart. You have touched a life.

Aglow Publications staff, for the work and support you gave me on this project.

SPECIAL THANKS:

To all the families who were willing to share their pains, problems, and triumphs for the benefit of others who need support. *Jigsaw Families* is by, about, and for all of you.

To Dr. Chuck James, Ph.D., for time, material, and special encouragement.

For those who are interested in contacting Dr. James for information on marriage seminars or counseling, please write: Church of the Nazarene, Counseling Center, 1644 Gault Street, Sumner, WA 98390.

Contents

Introduction

I have been married to my husband for nine years. I have never been remarried. Then again . . . maybe I have. Remarriage involves children as deeply as their parents. Perhaps more so.

My own parents were each married numerous times. With each marriage, they added to their hurt. My father left when I was six years old, and we didn't see him again for more than five years. The man who returned was much shorter than my daddy and a stranger. I lived with my mother, an older sister, and later a little brother.

My mother loved us and would do anything for us; she bought shoes for us when there were holes in her own. Looking back, I sometimes wonder if her marriages failed because she never found the "perfect father" for her children.

Were my parents bad people? I have always believed my mother was a good, loving person. Yet, in spite of all the love and support my mother gave me, the effects of living through the upheaval of multiple marriages still exist in parts of my life.

Ten years ago, I would have described my heart as brittle. I loved the Lord, but I held back parts of me even from him. My anger and bitterness toward my father boiled in spite of my mother's excuses for his behavior. Rather than abuse my father in his absence, my mother would tell me, "Michelle, he's your father. He loves you, and you should love him."

The Lord eventually healed my hurt and anger. I was stubborn and clung to my misery. The healing wasn't complete until after my father died.

Through my husband and God's love, I received a heart transplant. "I will give you a new heart and put a new spirit in you; I will remove from you your heart of stone and give you a heart of flesh" (Eze. 36:26).

My new heart is burdened for families struggling to make remarriage work. Fear of judgment isolates them from their Christian brothers and sisters. They often cry alone. Men cry on the way to work; women in a dark bedroom. They don't need words. They need support. They need hope. They need love.

1
...
The Incomplete Puzzle

Stranger watched the snowy-haired gentleman working intently at the large table. As he came closer, Stranger saw thousands of jigsaw puzzle pieces in jumbled array on the table. The old man, if he heard Stranger's approach, paid little attention. He vibrated with intensity. He mumbled to himself as he worked. Occasionally, he rubbed his eyes, sighed, or groaned. Stranger moved closer and saw the little man make small snips and clips on some of the puzzle pieces with a pair of scissors.

"Sir," Stranger interrupted, "why do you cut away the edges?"

The Old Man focused slowly on Stranger. "It's the only way. This is not one puzzle, but two. I found two puzzles, neither of which were complete by themselves. I am making a new picture."

Stranger thought for a moment. "But why not just throw them away? Surely they have no use now."

"I have use for them."

IDEALS

God has created an "ideal" man and "ideal" woman to love him, obey his word, and live in the freedom of doing his total will. These are ideals. The sad fact is that we disregard God's ideals. We sin. We disobey. We follow our own will. Only after we have waded through pain do we start to realize that God's ideal is often far from the reality that we create for ourselves through our disobedience.

Like the Lord, I have ideals for my children. One of those ideals is straight teeth. Yet, children fall short of having straight, healthy teeth in a number of ways.

"Nichole! Stop jumping on that bunk bed! If you fall off, you're going to get hurt!" A tape recorder would have proved as effective in halting Nichole's dangerous behavior. Even the memory of a spanking faded in the thrill of flying over the top bunk.

A solid thud shook the house. Then, an ominous quiet before the agonized cry began. I ran into the bedroom to find a bloody-faced Nichole sprawled on the carpet. In her Superwoman role, she flew off the top bunk and landed on her chin. Her teeth cut through her lip; one tooth was broken off.

I knew what would happen if she jumped on the bed. A typical mother, I reminded her all the way to the dentist about the times I'd told her not to play on the bunk beds. She still did it, and now she was hurt and would soon become an unwilling participant in a root canal procedure. Did she ever play on the bed again? You bet!

The Lord, as Creator, is the author of the principal of action and reaction. We do certain things that result in a positive or negative reaction. He tells us not to do things that cause negative reactions.

In Genesis, God gave the picture of ideal marriage. "For this reason a man will leave his father and mother and be united to his wife, and they will become one flesh" (Gen. 2:24). When asked about divorce, Jesus repeated God's Genesis message. Then he went on to say: "So they are no longer two, but one. Therefore what God has joined together, let man not separate" (Matt. 19:4-6). This is God's formula for well-being.

Jesus also gives acceptable reasons for divorce. For the last two thousand years, churches have held fervid debates about divorce. To start a food fight at the next potluck dinner, introduce the subject of a divorced Christian contemplating remarriage.

We must deal with this issue. Marriage is not an exception when it comes to man tiptoeing around God's commands. People divorce, and once divorced, it is common and acceptable in our society to remarry.

According to a 1981 survey of pastors, forty percent of families in our churches involve at least one person previously married. Right and wrong are for God to decide and his to forgive. But . . . right or wrong, the remarried couple and their families face a unique set of problems. Incredibly painful problems.

When Nichole hurt herself jumping off the bunk bed, I didn't pick up her tooth and say, "Here, fix it yourself. You shouldn't have jumped on the bed." I comforted her in her pain and did what I could to bring the tooth back to normalcy. Okay, okay, I *did* say, "I told you so." But God doesn't.

Families struggle to put pieces together from two different puzzles. Jesus tries to find as many missing puzzle pieces as he can. It's important for anyone who considers remarriage, after divorce or widowhood, to understand the complex process involved. No easy solutions to the problems quickly surface. There isn't even a picture to look at while the puzzle is worked. The original picture is a memory, not a guide.

IS REMARRIAGE RIGHT OR WRONG?

Can I condone or condemn remarriage? I could probably do both. Indeed, in my research for this book, I came across scripturally based books by pastors and counselors that both condemn and condone remarriage. The world does not need to hear one more opinion on the subject. What we need is an ear that hears what God wants to say to us.

Sometimes, as Christians, we presume that the only way God can voice right and wrong is through our own feeble mouths.

When my sister had some personal problems, I was sure of the root and solution to her trouble. I was sure God had given me the truth about her situation. At every opportunity I filled her ears with it. Like Job's friends, I gave her the best advice and complete with shaking finger, I said, "One of these days you'll be sorry!" I was so wise, the Lord had to move her one hundred eighty miles away before my strident voice could give way to his loving tone.

Later Cindy said, "You were right." But I wasn't. Jesus was right; I was loud.

Cindy found the help she needed in the Lord. I laugh now at the number of times I injected into our conversation, "I just want to say *one* thing . . ." then proceeded to impart some verbal gem. Cindy did need me. But she needed a sister who could quietly say, "I love you. And I know God loves you. Listen to him." I have learned so much since then. I can be that kind of sister now.

You and Jesus are the only ones who can truly examine

your decisions, both past and present. No man is your judge. "There is not a righteous man on earth who does what is right and never sins" (Eccles. 7:20). Seek the counsel of wise men, but base your decisions and your convictions on the Lord's counsel. He is the only one qualified as a judge. If you feel you made the wrong decision, admit it. Then take the final step—surrender.

SURRENDER

Even pain and misery are dear to us because they are ours. Maybe fear of retribution causes us to hang on to that last shred of self-control. Can *you* save your family? Can *you* bring change to your own life and then change others? Is that what you've been trying to do all along?

God loves you. He loves your family. Every piece of your family's puzzle is important to him. But if the pieces of your family are lost or bent, surrender your puzzle to him. Since Adam, God has worked in spite of man's independent personality. Put God in charge, and he'll make a new picture. His picture.

TIME TO CONSIDER

1. Are you certain of God's unbiased and immeasurable love for you? For your family?

2. Do you ever regret the decision to remarry? Why? Is regret accompanied by guilt? What is the source of the guilt?

3. Do you ever feel hurt or anger by the response or lack of understanding from people around you?

4. How do you feel about your marital relationship? About the Lord's role in your relationship?

2

...

The Right Pieces in the Wrong Puzzle

"I am in pain and distress; may your salvation, O God protect me" (Ps. 69:29).

Sharon stirred her coffee. "My first marriage lasted eleven years. It was almost five years later before I wanted anything to do with another man." A small laugh dispelled some of her tension. "It was an unhappy situation... another woman. My oldest son had leukemia, our daughter was three years old, and we had a two-month-old baby boy." She paused.

"Why did you eventually remarry?" I asked.

"I fell in love with Steven. I have a strong drive to be part of a family. I enjoy taking care of my home, and I love being a mother and wife. When I met Steven, we were just friends. After a year of friendship and casual dates, we knew we were in love and decided to get married."

"So, do you have the family you hoped for?"

As she swirled her coffee, Sharon shook her head. "It hasn't even begun to be what I hoped. There isn't the love, the caring, or the glue that holds a family together. I love Steven, and I know he loves me. But it takes a lot more than that."

There are few fairy tale marriages.

It should be easy, shouldn't it? A man and woman fall in love. They get married. Both people have children who either live with them or visit frequently. Actually, it becomes a group marriage. The new family moves into a big house, and as long as everyone is reasonable, problems sort themselves out. Right? Not necessarily!

When human beings are involved, nothing is reasonable or simple. David wrote the verse found at the beginning of this chapter. The words were the outpouring of an agonized heart. Here he was, God's anointed king. Once anointed, life should have been easy. He was in God's will and loved his Lord with a rare and beautiful passion. Yet enemies mocked him and scorned God. Two people whom David loved wanted to kill him. Life was and is complicated.

We long for a simpler life. Television creates for us what we can't have. A simple life. We compose fantasies; the fantasies become role models for reality.

THE BRADY BUNCH SYNDROME

The Brady Bunch became the role model for "blended families." Remember the theme song?

"Till the one day when the Lady met this fellow. And they knew it was much more than a hunch, that this group should somehow form a family, and that's the way they all became the Brady Bunch."

A woman with three girls, hair of gold, and four men

18

decide to become a family. The maid comes with the men. The family blends immediately into a family like any other on the block. It may be a little more crowded, but basically it's a happy, well-adjusted family. The girls call Mike, Dad; the boys call Carol, Mom. The problems they face have to do with fibbing, envy, birthday parties, and other minor squabbles.

As television entertainment, The Brady Bunch was a successful and popular comedy. The problems the two families faced were funny. Both parents carried out the duties of discipline with fairness and love. The maid, Alice, was loyal to both Mr. and Mrs. Brady and kept the big house and eight masters clean and in order. Never a question arose of children being treated prejudicially. No ex-spouses made unreasonable demands (because no ex-spouses appeared in the picture); in-laws and former in-laws evidently got along as well as the rest of the family. Even the dog was happy.

Reality and fantasy part company when reality is recognized. It's difficult to find two people who agree on discipline, housekeeping, animals, finances, and all the decisions involved in marriage and family life. In remarriages, there are often children, former husbands or wives, in-laws, and no maid. They are all involved in family matters to a certain degree. One woman told me, "Our family held summit meetings complete with a sergeant at arms to reach a solution on major decisions."

The Brady Bunch was fiction. A comedy. The non-fiction, dismal statistic in our country is that one out of two marriages end in divorce within ten years.[1] Eighty percent of divorced people remarry.[2] Sixty percent of the remarriages involve an adult with one or more children. Forty percent of second marriages end in divorce within four years. In 1979, over fifteen million children were living with a remarried parent.[3] By 1985, this number rose to twenty-five million.

HIGH EXPECTATIONS

Why do people remarry? Because the underlying hope or belief is that now that they have all this experience behind them, they'll do better the second (or third or fourth) time around. Their family will be Brady Bunch look-alikes. Sharon and Steven believed this.

"I really did assume too much. We didn't talk about discipline or bringing the family together. We thought we'd get married and life would follow a normal family pattern. Now, we can't even talk about the kids without a messy confrontation."

When two families blend, they try to put together an intricate puzzle with many wrong pieces. Traditional families consist of a mother, father, and however many children God gives them. The family follows a learning process to deal and communicate with one another. Conclusions or methods may not always be correct, but they are based on experience.

Consider this typical situation. Bobby gets home from elementary school at 4:00. Dinner is an hour away, but Bobby is hungry. He goes into the kitchen.

"Hi Mom. I'm hungry. Can I have a couple of cookies?" He is polite and relaxed.

"Okay, but you'd better eat all of your supper," she answers as she hands him the cookies.

Bobby's mother knows Bobby's eating habits. A couple of cookies won't spoil his appetite. Bobby knows Mom doesn't mind him having a snack after school. The situation is not a problem.

Two years later, Bobby's parents have divorced, and Bobby is living with his father. The bus drops Bobby off at

4:00, supper is eaten between 5:00 and 5:30, and Bobby's hungry. He goes into the kitchen.

"Hi Carla," he says to his stepmother. "I'm starved. Can I have a couple of cookies?"

Carla hesitates. "Bobby, it's awfully close to dinner time. I cooked something special. I think you'd better wait."

"Pleeease, I'm hungry now," Bobby pleads.

"Bobby, I said no. I don't want you to eat anything yet."

Bobby gets angry. "Man alive! My mom always let me have something to eat after school." He stomps out of the kitchen and up to his room to wait for his father.

Bobby and Carla are both angry and confused. Bobby's experience with his mother in similar matters led him to the conclusion that a snack after school was permissible. He can't see past his own confusion to recognize the effort Carla puts into a meal. She hopes to please and impress her new family with her culinary skills. Confusion turns to frustration and anger when other small differences in conditioning emerge.

The next day Bobby comes into the kitchen with Carla's two children. Unfortunately, Bobby forgot to wipe his feet.

"Bobby! How many times have I told you to wipe your feet before you come into the house? I am sick and tired of mopping floors just for you to come in and muddy them up!" Carla grabs an old towel and on her knees, wipes up the mess.

"Well, I'm sick and tired of you yelling at me! You don't yell at those guys like you do me!" Bobby flings his arm to indicate his stepbrother and stepsister. He crashes through the swinging kitchen door and again retreats to his room.

Bobby and Carla are not vindictive people. They are examples of just one problem that a jigsaw puzzle family faces, and they are only two pieces of a very large puzzle.

Before a first marriage, the engaged couple should have

a good idea of what it takes to make each other happy. At the same time, they strive to fulfill their own needs. Following marriage, the couple continues to grow and learn. They have a child and begin family life. From the day the child is born, he also begins the process of learning to manipulate and relate to his parents and caretakers. The parents go through a day-by-day College of Child Psychology that enables them to understand and deal with their child.

Divorce and remarriage change the pieces of the puzzle. Suddenly Bobby and Carla must start all over again. Their individual procedures and customs differ radically. Confusion and anger is inevitable.

How can they sort it all out?

THE WISDOM OF SOLOMON

King Solomon requested of the Lord, "So give your servant a discerning heart to govern your people and to distinguish between right and wrong" (1 Kings 3:9). Solomon asked God for wisdom for one reason—he could not make crucial decisions without *supernatural* wisdom. God granted his request, and his discernment became legendary.

If you are remarried, you need supernatural wisdom. It won't make you infallible. Solomon made many blunders. But the more you depend on God's wisdom, the less you will feel the strain of responsibility. He was not ashamed to admit his lack of knowledge and ask for God's help. He hungered for understanding. Are you hungry?

ASSUME NOTHING

Many people, such as Sharon and her husband, get married and assume the love they feel for each other will be contagious. Their children will love their "new mother" or their "new father"; the new spouse will feel deep affection for the stepchildren. Of course, the dog will love them all.

A marriage and a stepfamily can last. What you learned during your first marriage *can* be used to build a stronger relationship. But first, be honest with yourself, your spouse, the children, and most of all, with the Lord. Making a marriage work requires prayer, sweat, tears, self-denial, and oceans of understanding. At times, only one partner will be interested in the effort. Some children will be left angry and bitter for the rest of their lives. Maybe not at you, but you will bear the heat of their bitterness nonetheless.

Can such a union survive? Yes. Can happiness reside in your home? Yes. Jehovah is the master of impossible odds.

You have a better chance for survival than Jonah did. When thrown into the sea, a huge fish came along and swallowed him whole. Surely he would die for his disobedience to the Lord. For three days and three nights Jonah was inside the fish. Did he have any assurance that he would survive this ordeal? Did the Lord appear and say, "Do not fear, this is just a detour to Ninevah"?

Jonah waited for death. And as he waited, he prayed:

When my life was ebbing away,
I remembered you, Lord,
and my prayer rose to you,
to your Holy Temple.
Those who cling to worthless idols
forfeit the grace that could be theirs.
But I, with a song of thanksgiving,
will sacrifice to you.
What I have vowed I will make good.
Salvation comes from the Lord
(Jonah 2:7-9).

Salvation did come. "The Lord commanded the fish and, it vomited Jonah onto dry land" (Jonah 2:10).

There is hope. Be patient. God will use the right pieces and reshape the wrong ones to fit.

Even when you think some of those pieces hate you.

TIME TO CONSIDER

"And the God of all grace, who called you to his eternal glory in Christ, after you have suffered a little while, will himself restore you and make you strong, firm and steadfast" (1 Pet. 5:10).

1. Apply the above verse to your situation. What is your *instinctive* reaction? Can you accept this verse in a personal way, written for you?

2. What were your expectations when you married the *first* time? How do they differ from your expectations for your restructured family?

3. How well has your present marriage fulfilled your initial expectations? What surprises did the relationship hold for you?

4. Did you have hidden resentments that surfaced in your second marriage? What was the source (or sources) of your resentment? Who bore the brunt of it?

5. What do you need from your present marital relationship? What do you perceive to be your spouse's needs?

6. How has remarriage affected you spiritually? What have you asked the Lord to do in your marriage?

3
...

Help!
They Hate Me!

The old man worked on the puzzle, and Stranger watched, mesmerized. The small light over the table provided dim illumination, and Stranger's eyes hurt. Engrossed in the old man's efforts, he found himself still watching as the sun melted into the sill below the window. No words were spoken. Minute clippings formed a thin layer of debris on the floor where they fell. The task would seem dreary were it not for the passion of the laborer.

Stranger detected a subtle shift in the old man's position. His silver brows furrowed as his hands tried to place a piece in the puzzle, only to withdraw and snip again at the edges. It wouldn't fit. After several attempts, the puzzle piece finally met the surrounding edges but not without obvious gaps.

"What has happened? Why is this piece harder to fit

than others?" Stranger's question broke the silence.

As the old man lifted his head, he closed his eyes. He did not open them to look at Stranger. He brought his hands to his temples and massaged in a circular motion. Was it the strain? Or did sadness muffle the reply?

"Some of the puzzle has been damaged. A few pieces were only slightly torn and easily mended. But this piece was scratched and gouged, the beautiful colors distorted by pain. I had to create a new shape, and I grieve each cut I made. The loss was great."

Stranger pondered a moment. "You have so many pieces. Why must an imperfect piece be included in the puzzle?"

The old man's eyes opened. He gazed into and through Stranger. "No piece is perfect, but each is essential."

THE ONLY PERFECT PIECE

My anticipation to reach heaven is not based on streets of gold, or treasures, or even a mansion. I can't wait to ask questions. My eternity will be full of questions to the Lord and to people in the Bible. I suppose I'll have to wait in line to speak with Mary and Joseph, but it will be worth the wait.

Maybe we'll sit in the grass under a beautiful, ageless tree and talk about Jesus. I've always been curious about the child Jesus. How did he learn to talk? When did he learn to walk? How many times did he have to be told to stay away from the fire?

When I started this book, a new curiosity developed. It occurred to me that Jesus was, technically, a stepchild. No great, in-depth theological expositories exist to prove or disprove my theory. But I believe Joseph, Mary, and Jesus empathize with jigsaw families. I think they understand the pain.

The apostle Luke was sensitive to heart issues. He told the story about Mary and Joseph accidentally leaving Jesus behind in Jerusalem. As mothers, we know the flood of panic and anguish when our children are missing; the deluge of relief when we see their faces and know they're safe. After a frantic three-day search, Mary and Joseph found Jesus in the temple. They ran in, grabbed him by the shoulders, and said (paraphrased), "What are you doing?! We've been looking everywhere for you! We were worried sick!"

Jesus' answer was calm and to the point. "Why were you searching for me?" he asked. "Didn't you know I had to be in my father's house?" (Luke 2:48,49).

As far as Mary and Joseph were concerned, *they* were Jesus' mother and father. They raised him. They were responsible for him. But Jesus set himself apart. He knew his real Father, and his first priority was this relationship.

We don't know how Joseph felt. Or Jesus. We know Jesus was perfect and obedient. We know he gained the respect of God and people. But were there times of pain and stress? Did Joseph feel "left out" of Jesus' life or emotions? Did the child Jesus ever feel like he didn't belong? Misunderstood?

A part of me, maybe the fanciful part, says he did. And he understands how you feel. He feels the frustration and the ache you feel. He goes through the pain with you.

A TIME TO CRY

Brenda aches all over. Her head throbs from unshed tears. Her stomach is clenched with stress. Brenda's heart sits like lead within her chest as Tom's words replay in her mind.

"I hate you! I can't stand you, and I wish my dad never married you!" Tom, Brenda's "new son," screamed with every inch of his twelve-year-old body. Then he ran to his room.

Brenda sits in the bedroom she shares with Tom's father and aches.

Why does Tom hate me?

UNDERSTANDING THE CHILD

Is Tom a spoiled, obnoxious little boy who is desperately trying to break up his father's marriage? It's possible. There *are* spoiled, obnoxious children in the world who make trouble for trouble's sake. But in Tom's case, the problems run deeper. He is a child involved in the complexities of second marriage.

Let's go back to before Tom's father married Brenda. Tom didn't understand why his mom and dad divorced. His dad sat down with him one day, and the expression on his dad's face made Tom's throat constrict.

"Hey buddy, I wanted to tell you something. First of all, I love you. You know that, don't you? But I'm afraid I can't live here at home anymore." Tom's blue eyes widened. "It's so hard to explain son, but Mom and I just don't love each other. Not the way a husband and wife should, anyway. We want you to know, though, this has nothing to do with you. We both love you very much. We will always love you."

"But Daddy!" Tom started to cry. He didn't understand. His father comforted him as much as he could. He told him about all the great things they would do together on weekends. He kidded him about the "bachelor dinners" in an apartment somewhere. Then, with a tight hug, Daddy left. He left a hole that gapes inside Tommy. A hole Tom can't see or understand.

Life begins to change.

THE HURRICANES OF CHANGE

In the intact nuclear family, a child experiences and deals with an astonishing number of changes. Attending the first day of school, he faces strangers alone. Later, a family move means a child must start all over again in a new school. When children hit puberty, they are thrown into a bedlam of confused feelings and emotions. Bodies change. Ideas form in their heads independent of their parents' thinking.

And dating! Boys face the fear of rejection. Girls feel awkward and inferior if they spend Friday and Saturday nights eating popcorn and reading a book. If they don't want to date, they are afraid something is wrong with them. In high school, they try to decide what to do with the rest of their lives while dealing with sexual pressure, homework, and often a job. Wow!

I listed only some of the major changes a child faces within a twelve-year span. Add to this list the following problems:

Gerry

When Gerry was six years old, she witnessed her father threatening her mother with a knife. "I'm going to cut you into pieces!" he growled drunkenly while his two daughters cowered on the stairs.

Later, when he was sober, her father explained, "Your mother and I don't love each other anymore. But we will always love you."

He didn't hear her six-year-old mind say, *"If Daddy can stop loving Mommy, he can stop loving me. Will Daddy cut me with a knife?"*

Sheila

The first time thirteen-year-old Sheila saw her mother and stepfather enter a bedroom together, she felt a combination of shame, embarrassment, and jealousy. She doesn't understand *why*, but Sheila feels like a stranger in her own home.

Allen

Allen lived with his father and brother for two years after his parents' divorce. Then his dad married a woman with two daughters. Allen is fourteen, and one of his stepsisters is thirteen. His father and stepmother treat them as brother and sister. They don't realize Allen has developed an infatuation for Alicia. He doesn't know how to handle his feelings and is too embarrassed to admit them to his father. Confusion over his relationship with his stepsister, his inability to talk with his dad, and shame makes Allen angry and difficult to live with.

Rapid changes combined with the reconditioning process discussed in chapter two often produces a child who is angry, confused, and resentful. According to the child's individual character, resentment is poured out in spurts and gushes or in abrasive undercurrents.

Does Tom hate Brenda? Unless Brenda has done something calloused or mean, Tom very likely projects his anger onto Brenda. Tom's father could have married anyone, and the reaction would be as vehement. This fact is irrelevant to Brenda and Tom as they face their painful predicament. Tom's piece of the puzzle is essential to the whole. He can be a force for destruction or a bonding agent.

THE HELP

Good news is available for every stepparent. *DON'T*

GIVE UP. There is hope, and there is help. You can have a house that doesn't require a land-mine detector to walk safely through. However, keep in mind some of the realities.

Some puzzle pieces, some children, have been bent and so hurt they will never be the same. Children who have experienced physical, sexual, or emotional abuse must have counseling. The whole family should be involved with a competent counselor. Even when a child seems to be functioning well, deep-rooted fears and rages often boil inside.

You can take some basic steps to help your jigsaw family come together with fewer gaps. These steps are a process. Nothing of lasting value has been created overnight since Genesis. Rebuilding one family out of the remains of two requires prayer, commitment, prayer, sweat, prayer, and time.

1) *Pray.* You've heard the cliché, "All I can do now is pray." Is prayer a last resort? David's greatest strength was his willingness to fall to his knees. He knew he could not help himself. The Psalms are verbal images of a man who cried for help. And received it.

When you pray, be honest. Don't tell God you love your difficult stepdaughter if you don't. The Lord knows you, and he knows the child. If you can't be honest about your feelings, then you are still making excuses for them. Honesty with yourself and the Lord allows him to work in you and to change you.

2) *Examine yourself.* Am I trying, albeit with good intentions, to change the child? Dr. Chuck James, family counselor and associate pastor at Sumner Church of the Nazarene, Sumner, Washington, states, "One of the worst things a stepparent can do is try to improve a child. Of course the child resents the stepparent. A new adult moves into the house and begins to discipline; the child becomes

confused and angry. He sees no basis for this person's claim to authority."

If you want to improve your relationship with your stepchildren, accept them. Accept their nail biting. Accept their chewing with their mouths open like hungry birds. Accept them as they are with warts, pimples, and attitudes intact.

We all need acceptance. My husband Gordon married someone who is not "just like Mom." Me. It is only natural that he would want me to exhibit the qualities he admired in his mother. She was a wonderful woman. I have good qualities, but I also have traits that disqualify me for the "Mother of the Year" award. Gordon could try to change me, but he doesn't. He's smart. I have strong reactions to someone trying to reshape me.

3) *Listen*. In my interview with Dr. James, I asked him what *one* thing would make the biggest difference in relieving tension in subsequent marriage homes. His reply was enveloped in a single word: "*Listen*. There is not a family in the world that would not benefit by learning to listen."

A child cannot resist an adult who listens. As a stepparent, you have the potential to form a friendship with the children in your family. Ask relevant questions, and hear the answers.

4) *Love unconditionally*. Ashley admitted she didn't love her stepson. For two years she'd felt guilty about her inability to love this boy. One day the Lord told her a secret. She didn't have to love her stepson; Jesus does it for her.

Ashley stopped trying to manufacture her emotions. She concentrated on letting her stepson know, in little ways, that Jesus loved him. No matter what.

The young man found notes in his lunchbox that said, "Jesus always cares" and "Neither height not depth, nor anything else in all creation, will be able to separate us from the love of God that is in Christ Jesus our Lord" (Rom. 8:39).

At first, the boy looked at Ashley like she had purple hair. And Ashley still felt frustrated. But a thin cord was being woven between them. A bond born out of Jesus' love. A bond strengthened because it does not depend on human emotion. When the Lord released Ashley from her guilt, he freed her to love out of choice instead of duty.

5) *Be supportive.* Both parents should sit down, without children present, and discuss a support system. This is a time to refrain from accusations or "pointing out." The system is simple in theory; difficult in practice. Each person agrees that no matter what the other parent says to a child, they will back each other up in front of the child.

We all deal with various situations differently. When a disparity in discipline arises, the adults quietly adjourn to another part of the house to discuss it. If a change is agreed upon, then the responsible parent returns to the child and confesses, "I've changed my mind."

This support system is not built overnight. But it may save your marriage. It takes the child out of the middle. He can't play both sides against each other.

6) *Develop sensitivity.* Look for ways to avoid uncomfortable situations inside the family. Don't throw male and female stepchildren into the same house without discussing new rules of mutual privacy. If you sense a child is hurt or confused, don't ignore him. Sit down with the children, and give them a chance to talk openly about feelings. You don't need to tell them they are right or wrong to feel the way they do. Just listen.

The suggestions in this chapter aren't all inclusive and won't cover every possible situation. But they can alter some of the feelings of helplessness. Keep in mind that according to most counselors, it takes a year and a half to two years to establish parental responsibilities in the family.[1]

You are essential to your family puzzle. Your child, no matter how bitter and angry, is also essential to the puzzle. But in spite of all your best efforts, some children will not, or maybe cannot, respond to you or the Lord. These children require a special attitude: "I'll do my best, and give God the rest."

Jesus was perfect. His incredible love sent him to a cross. Can you love more than that? Yet many people rejected his love. In Mark 3, we're told Jesus' own family thought he was out of his mind. Some people won't respond to you. It hurts. But you can't change them.

Do what you know the Lord wants *you* to do. Leave everything else to him.

Then, just when you think you've found all the pieces to your puzzle, a new box is uncovered, and guess what's inside? A whole bunch of extra pieces!

TIME TO CONSIDER

1. What should your role be in your family? Do you feel restricted in the exercise of that role? How?

2. How do you support your spouse when it comes to family discipline? How can you improve your level of support?

3. What is the marital relationship like apart from the children?

4. Do you consider yourself a good spiritual role model for your children and stepchildren? Why or why not?

4

...

Extra People

Remarriage resembles a tire with bulges in the rubber. The tire still rolls, but the ride is bumpy. Ex-spouses are one of the bulges in the tire of remarriage. Even when the protrusion isn't visible, the evidence is there.

Jacob had so many bumps on his wheel I'm surprised his teeth didn't rattle loose. His marital story begins in Genesis 29. Tricked into marriage to his first wife Leah, he married Rachel a week later. The Bible tells us Jacob loved Rachel more than Leah. But when Leah started having babies, Rachel grew insecure and jealous. So Rachel told Jacob, "Give me children, or I'll die!" (Gen. 30:1).

It's difficult to be reasonable when you're jealous.

Rachel brought Bilhah her maidservant to Jacob and asked him to give her children through Bilhah. Leah, reluctant to fall behind, brought her own maid Zilpah to Jacob's tent for procreation.

Then, one sunny day, Leah's oldest son brought her some mandrake plants he'd found.

"Rachel said to Leah, 'Please give me some of your son's mandrakes.'

"But she said to her, 'Wasn't it enough that you took away my husband? Will you take my son's mandrakes too?'

" 'Very well,' Rachel said, 'he can sleep with you tonight in return for your son's mandrakes.'

"So when Jacob came in from the fields that evening, Leah went out to meet him. 'You must sleep with me,' she said. 'I have hired you with my son's mandrakes.' So he slept with her that night" (Gen. 30:14-16).

Who was in the middle? Was anyone happy? Jacob himself became a source of competition with children as trophies.

Jacob's life was not so different from many remarriages today. I don't think he expected the rivalry and bitterness that developed in his family.

People enter remarriage with reasonable expectations; the relationship with the person they dated will remain much the same. Life will continue along the same path, except instead of running between two residences, the path starts at the front door of the marriage cottage. They believe the "other" family is important but in the background.

In her book *Second Wife, Second Best?* Glynnis Walker says, "It is a peculiar reality that many men leave their families and focus their attention on finding new wives, but once they have them, their attention reverts to their established responsibilities."[1] To some degree, this applies to both remarried men and women. The marriage contract can be legally severed, but the emotional bonds remain intact.

In my research, I came across many books on divorce

and remarriage. Many authors wrote from personal experience. They were bitter and angry at those whom they had once loved enough to marry. In spite of their post-marital wrath, one bubble of truth kept floating to the surface: the ties that bind are stronger than legal paper and judicial decrees.

The Bible explains the bond that exists between married people: "For this reason a man will leave his father and mother and be united to his wife, *and they will become one flesh*" (Gen. 2:24 italics added).

Nature and all its intricacies bear witness to God's poetic essence. But when he said "and they will become one flesh," he was not being poetic. The passage describes a process couples go through after the wedding. Intricate cords are woven out of shared experiences, tragedies, and parenthood. Even divorce, traumatic and angry though it may be, is part of this bond.

My mother and father's marriage was painful and turbulent. They divorced when I was six years old. They both married again, more than once. Fifteen years after their bitter divorce, my father died. I was surprised by my mother's reaction. She wept. Her tears were born, in part, of compassion. But her ache was for the husband, the father, and the broken dreams that still hung by a thread.

A new spouse must accept the existence of former marital ties. Such acceptance rarely takes place immediately or on a permanent basis. It is difficult to be rational about "marital ties" when you fear the loss of love and family. And every time you think your insecurity is vanquished, a new situation arises. The new spouse must deal repeatedly with jealousy, hurt, and resentment—the same emotions Leah and Rachel struggled with throughout their married lives.

ONE STEP AT A TIME

Our first son died when he was two-and-a-half-months old. He was diagnosed as a Sudden Infant Death Syndrome victim. Three months after his death, I became pregnant with my daughter Nichole, the bunk-bed acrobat. My obstetrician and pediatrician both expressed concern. They felt I had not had enough time between Jason's death and a new pregnancy to cope with anxiety.

I knew fear would be my companion. It was a natural reaction. But I also knew I did not want fear to control my life or how I raised this next child.

After Nichole's birth, each time I looked into the crib panic squeezed my lungs. The moment sickening fear burst into my brain, the Lord whispered in my ear, "Your feelings are natural, but we *can* get past them."

The Psalms became personal to me. "I sought the Lord, and he answered me; he delivered me from all my fears" (Ps. 34:4).

I didn't become a Super Christian. No *constant* peace shut out fear or anguish. God never guaranteed my daughter would live. I was just a young mother who learned that God is always nearby, and all I had to do was turn to him.

Instead of a decision never to be afraid, I dealt with my fear each time it appeared. Likewise, when you marry a divorced person, you will have to deal with your feelings about the ex-spouse one step at a time. Make a decision not to let your insecurities control your marriage.

TRIPLE TRIANGULATION

Jigsaw families often become so extended, the family members lose their sense of belonging. The family that once provided an anchor now tosses like the sea itself. To understand how far a family can spread itself after divorce and subsequent marriages, let's look at the increased family structure.

Phyllis and George are unhappy and decide to divorce. Matters are settled. They are no longer husband and wife.

Eventually Phyllis, who has custody of their three children, marries Ron. Ron is also divorced and shares joint custody of his three children with his ex-wife who is also remarried.

George meets Dana, who agrees to marry him. His new wife has two children by her former husband.

Within this structure, six adults must work out visitation. Eight children wonder who they'll spend Christmas with this year. How far can this go? As far as the imagination! (See diagram, fig. 1.)

This example shows the result of one divorce per person for each of the significant adults. When one or more of the adults has more than one divorce, the whole diagram is enlarged.

All of this sounds like a soap opera. But then, where do you think soap operas get their material?

In Jamie Keshet's *Love and Power in the Stepfamily: a Practical Guide*, she quotes a father who is caught in the triple triangle of visiting children, ex-spouses, and new spouses. He said, "I am expected to change my plans because my ex-wife's second husband's ex-wife's mother is ill."[2]

Sometimes, the triangle takes a new angle. Friendships form in place of bitterness. The results are never predictable.

DARLA AND ALEX AND TINA

Darla married Alex two years ago. Although they are happy, Darla often feels jealous of her husband's dedication to his work. Alex's former wife Tina frequently brings

Jigsaw Families

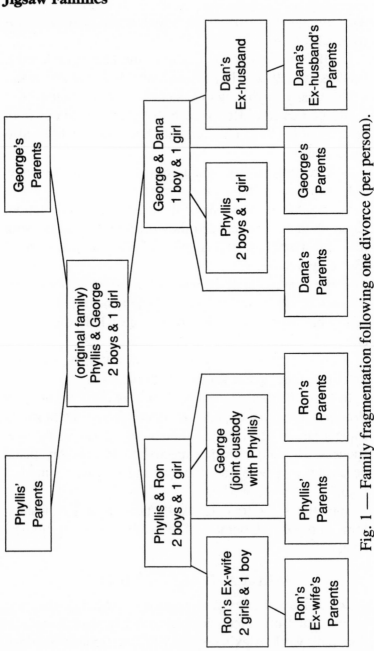

Fig. 1 — Family fragmentation following one divorce (per person).

Alex's children to the house. Darla finds herself drawn to Tina's pleasant personality and easy warmth. Before long, Tina and Darla begin to call each other on the telephone just to chat. It was inevitable that the chats stray to Alex.

"Oh Darla," Tina sympathizes, "I hoped he wouldn't be that way with you."

Such sympathy can have a positive and negative effect. While Darla received support from her friend, Alex felt outnumbered. It made him uncomfortable to think his wives were comparing notes. But since he thought there might be advantages to the two women being on good terms, he never said anything. He just withdrew from Darla.

How many marital problems would be solved if a wife could talk to her husband the way she talks to her closest friend? In fairness to the husbands of the world, what would happen if the wife *would* talk to her husband *before* she talked to her friend?

Communication. It's a two-way wire.

THE INTERFERING SPOUSE

In chapter two, I talked about the Brady Bunch Syndrome. One interesting facet of the old comedy was the missing parents. As far as I know, their absence was never explained.

Was Carol's former husband caught in an avalanche in Turkey? Maybe he survived but has amnesia and can't find his way back to California. And poor Mike. His wife slipped into anonymity as completely and mysteriously as Carol's husband.

There may have been an episode that explained that both Mike and Carol were widowed. But even if a former spouse dies, there are residual affects. Especially for the children. Yet the children never mentioned their respective lost parents. They never seemed to feel disloyal to their real mother or father. Mike and Carol both entered marriage free of former spouses or their memories.

All of this is to make a point, of course. The majority of jigsaw families involve at least one extra adult. There is enough hostility in the thought of an ex-spouse to inspire some entrepreneur to make bumper stickers that read: "Ex-wife (or husband) in trunk." Many people are vindictive and angry when it comes to former relationships.

Betty told her story, "John's ex-wife called at all hours. It didn't matter to her if it was 3:00 a.m. or not. Dorothy left John in the first place because she was having an affair. She wanted to marry the man. But now that John and I are married, she's jealous. I think she can't stand the thought of us in bed together."

One night, Dorothy managed to enter John and Betty's home while they were out. When they returned, the curtains hung in shreds, furniture was turned over, and dishes broken. At first they thought there had been a burglary, but nothing was stolen. John called Dorothy and began to tell her about the mess.

"You know I did it. Why don't you just say it?" she said.

John couldn't believe it. "You did it?" He paused as anger surged, "Why? Why would you do something like this?" he yelled.

"I made a mess of your house like you made a mess of my life." Dorothy was so calm it enraged John even more.

"I could have you thrown in jail!"

"Explain that one to your kids." The click on the other end told John the conversation was over. Betty cried softly in the bedroom, and John stood with the telephone receiver still in his hand. He was dumbfounded.

No one called the police. Betty and John cleaned the house, called a locksmith to change the locks, and waited.

They wondered what else Dorothy might do. Her actions were not rational, and it frightened them.

Stories like John and Betty's are not uncommon.

LOOKING FORWARD

A friend who is engaged to marry a divorced man read this chapter of my manuscript. Her pensive eyes looked at me over the pages. "Is this what I have to look forward to?"

I didn't have an answer for her. Or maybe I do.

Another friend of mine, Suzie, was given a baby shower near the end of her first pregnancy. While the cake was passed, one of the mothers present began to describe her first delivery. The vivid tale included thirty-three hours of labor, a group of student doctors, and stitches, which by her graphic description, must have run right up to her nose.

The mother-to-be sat in disbelief and shock. "Why didn't someone tell me this before?" she breathed.

"Oh honey!" quipped another friend, "Don't you worry. You won't go through all that. Why, my water broke and twenty minutes later I had a baby boy. I didn't even have a chance to say 'hee-hee-hoo.' " She referred to the method of pain relief used in Lamaze delivery.

Suzie looked at her. "It takes us at least thirty minutes to get to the hospital." A deep frown puckered her forehead. "We'll never make it."

Finally, someone with common sense spoke up. Grandma Garsee's soft voice came from a corner of the room. "Suzie, the Lord knows how long you need to get to the hospital. He knows when the baby will be ready. And he knows you. Worry about when the baby will come or how long it will take won't change a thing. But it will make the time you have left long and miserable. Each birth is a different experience. You'll cope with yours just by following God's plan for you."

Suzie's fears receded.

Like birthing a baby, no two marriages are alike. No pat answer fits every situation.

My engaged friend may face many of the problems covered in this book. Or she might not.

My advice to her was this: "Prepare yourself mentally, emotionally, and spiritually to do your best. God knows you; he knows your fiancé. Worrying about what might happen won't change a thing. Except you."

With extra people, the puzzle is complicated by the many pieces. But *all* puzzles must be put together one piece at a time.

My two-year-old has a puzzle. We put it together one piece at a time. All seven pieces.

The pieces of your puzzle and the problems you face in your family: finances, your spouse, extra people—everything—must be placed in the puzzle one piece at a time. You can't "solve" one problem without working on another. The pieces are interdependent. Interlocking.

If you haven't found answers to your questions yet, don't be discouraged. A puzzle always makes more sense when it is seen as a whole. Sometimes a puzzle has us so confused, we no longer know how to finish it. Or we wonder *if* we want to finish it.

One woman told me, "I don't even know how to pray anymore or if I want my marriage saved. I am so tired, I don't know what I want." The Lord understands us so well. He is the one who translates our groans into prayers. "In the same way, the Spirit helps us in our weakness. We do not know what we ought to pray, but the Spirit himself intercedes for us with groans that words cannot express" (Rom. 8:26).

HEART DISEASE

Bitterness is heart disease with a seeping contagion. The rivalry begun between Leah, Rachel, Bilhah, and Zilpah did not die with them. Resentment spilled over and took root in the hearts of their children and blossomed into a plan of murder. The brothers settled for selling Joseph to slave traders.

God used the product and result of bitterness to build a nation. But it didn't happen instantly. Joseph suffered incredible pain and loss on his way to Pharoah's court. Inside the man equal in power to Pharoah was a frightened, homesick boy, sold into slavery by his own brothers.

Time belongs to God. It was by the Lord's watch that Joseph was reunited with his family. At a preset hour, Joseph was able to interpret Pharoah's dream.

Can you wait as long as Joseph did? Can you work in the prison until you are invited to the palace?

So far, we have worked on the inside of our puzzle.

We still need some important pieces. We haven't touched the in-laws, or the ex-laws. Next we'll explore the fancy stuff.

TIME TO CONSIDER

1. How do you feel when you deal with an ex-spouse? (Either your own or your partner's.) Is there a sense of competition? In what way?

2. Think about your own ex-spouse for a moment. Make a list of the emotions evoked by the thought of that person. How do those feelings affect your present life?

3. Read 2 Corinthians 12:7-10. Who or what is the thorn in your flesh? How can God use your thorn(s)?

Jigsaw Families

I heard Dr. Benjamin Reed tell about his early days in the ministry. Those first difficult years taught him that there are basically two kinds of people: those who are good *to* you, and those who are good *for* you. The people who are good *to* you help, love, and encourage you. People who are good *for* you drive you to your knees before God pleading for his guidance. The extra time with the Lord is good for you.

4. What kind of ex-spouse are you?

5
...

In-laws, Ex-laws, and Other Fancy Stuff

A question ran unbidden and unanswered through Stranger's mind. "Why am I still here? I sit here hour after hour and watch an old man work a puzzle that will probably never be whole."

The old man's voice startled Stranger. "Do you want to leave?"

"Yes," Stranger said quietly.

"Why don't you?" the old man's tone was not unkind. Just curious.

"I can't. I don't know why I can't leave. I just can't." Stranger waited. A thought crossed his mind. "You know why I can't leave. Don't you?"

The old man's only reply was a shift in expression and a change of subject. "You know, I actually enjoy this part of the puzzle. Edges give the picture continuity and shape."

His expression matched his light tone and words. He seemed younger. Happier. As Stranger watched, a border began to take shape around the fringes of the ragged puzzle. He even recognized a piece that seemed just right for a spot at the top of the picture.

"I don't mean to interfere, but would this piece fit the space at the top?" he asked, pointing at the small shape.

"You may try placing the piece, if you like." The old man continued to work on another section of the puzzle. In the gentle hours of evening, Stranger worked beside him.

FANCY SPICES

My husband and I were still newlyweds when Daryl and Julie, a couple from North Carolina, visited us for a week. Julie was the first person who ever made me feel like a gourmet cook. Come to think of it, Julie was the last person who made me feel like a gourmet cook.

As a young wife, I was still trying to convince myself that I *loved* to cook. One afternoon, Julie kept me company in the kitchen while I made potato salad. Usually I forgot to put in one or more of the ingredients in anything I cooked so I was nervous about this new attempt. I remembered I had included potatoes so I was assured of at least partial success. As I added more ingredients, my house guest began a taste test on the salad. With her fingers. Repeatedly. Without washing them.

With two fingers, Julie scooped up a mushy potato from the middle of the bowl, and in a single motion popped it into her mouth. "Umm, that's good!" she purred while she licked the dressing from her fingers. Then she scooped again. As a diversion, I moved the bowl to another counter, closer to the spices. She followed me.

"What're ya doin' over here?" Julie asked as her hand descended into the bowl once more.

"I need to put in the salt and pepper," I answered. I tried not to be offended by her casual kitchen manners.

"What for?"

"I haven't put any in yet," I said, a little confused. I shook the salt container vigorously over the salad, and did the same with the pepper.

"Oh no!" Julie's face showed alarm and disappointment. "You've ruined it! When I make potato salad, I leave it plain. I never use any *fancy* spices." Julie's fingers stayed out of my bowl.

In-laws, ex-laws, and all the friends and relatives that come with old and new marriages become one of two things: the "fancy spices" that add flavor and variety to your family or the fingers that won't stay out of your bowl.

Most in-laws (and ex-laws) represent a little of both. But whether in-laws represent spice or dirty fingers, they definitely make up the outer edges of your family puzzle. Good or bad, they are a necessary part of the fringes. It is desirable that these fringes form an attractive border to enhance the whole picture.

The Bible gives us a look at dirty fingers and fragrant spices. Genesis tells us about Laban, and Ruth describes Naomi.

Leah and Rachel were Laban's daughters. Laban knew of Jacob's intense love for Rachel; Jacob willingly worked seven years to earn the right to marry Laban's younger daughter. Seven years Jacob worked and dreamed of the wedding night. Seven years and one day later he awoke next to Leah, Rachel's older sister.

He was upset.

"What is this you have done to me? I served you for Rachel, didn't I? Why have you deceived me?"

Laban replied, "It is not our custom here to give the younger daughter in marriage before the older one. Finish this daughter's bridal week: then we will give you the younger one also, in return for another seven years of work" (Gen. 29:25-27).

Laban's deception was cruel. It hurt everyone involved. Jacob worked in bondage to his father-in-law for fourteen years. Leah married a man who loved another woman and made no secret of it. Rachel became the "second wife" one week following Leah's big marriage feast. Laban was a terrible father-in-law.

A book of balances, the Bible also talks about good in-laws. The book of Ruth is a story of a mother-in-law who loved her daughters-in-law. Naomi referred to Ruth and Orpah as daughters. The close relationship between the three women is obvious in the moment Naomi tells the two younger women to return to their own families.

"Then Naomi said to her two daughters-in-law, 'Go back each of you, to your mother's home. May the Lord show kindness to you, as you have shown to your dead and to me. . . .'

"Then she kissed them and they wept aloud and said to her, 'We will go back with you to your people' " (Ruth 1:9-10).

Ruth's insistence in going to Bethlehem with Naomi was not born out of duty. It was an act of great love for her mother-in-law. Such love is earned.

The majority of in-laws and ex-laws share a basic desire to see their children happy. If they believe you can make their child happy, you will be accepted. If they believe you will cause their child unhappiness, you have a problem. Where former in-laws are concerned, it's natural that they will side with their own child. Not always. But most of the time.

TOUGH QUESTIONS

Sit down with a piece of paper, and write out the kind of relationship you desire with your fringe people. Those puzzle pieces that form the edges.

Do you want sincere friendship? You don't have to. We often assume we must have an intimate friendship with everyone we meet, and it's true God wants us to love the people around us. But friendship is a reciprocal relationship, a give *and* take of love, support, and empathy.

Jesus loves people enough to die for them. This is Christ's love en masse. But in John 11 is a picture of the special relationship Jesus had with Mary, Martha, and Lazarus. He loved them; he hurt with them; he was moved by them. Jesus loves all men, but he was friends with Mary, Martha, and Lazarus.

The relationship Ruth and Naomi shared was reciprocal. Each one earned the love and respect of the other. Beyond kinship, Ruth and Naomi were bound by friendship.

Do you want to "get along" with your fringe people? For many people in remarriage, to "get along" with in-laws and old family friends would be a relief. This is not a bad goal. Considering the emotional roller coaster of divorce, the "get along" option may be the most obtainable goal. Or it would make an excellent jumping-off point.

Do you want to discontinue contact with your ex-spouse's family and friends? This isn't unusual so don't feel guilty about it. But do analyze it honestly. Your family unit has expanded considerably. It can be quite a chore to keep in contact with such a large group of people. Are your feelings based on convenience? Or are there bitter roots to your problem?

Carefully consider the children involved before you break contact with grandparents. In such a situation, the losers are the children. Those who may already feel rejected by their non-custodial parent may assume their grandparents have also rejected them. Whenever possible, preserve your child's sense of family continuity.

How would your family benefit from improved communication with in-laws and former in-laws? Is there a potential for negative results? Ellen's ex-husband had sexually molested their daughter for two years. Ellen made the decision to cut off communication between her children and their biological grandparents. The court granted Ellen full custody of the children; the father disappeared.

"My former in-laws live in the same town we do. They constantly call and ask the children to come to their house. But my ex-husband's parents don't believe he did anything wrong. I'm afraid of what they might say to the children." Ellen, very determined, added, "My children were hurt deeply. I won't knowingly allow anyone to hurt them or confuse them again."

Ellen's decision to end her family's relationship with her former in-laws has its roots in both an emotional and a rational vein. It's understandable. She is protecting her children who have been tragically betrayed. But there may be a way she can let her children maintain a bond with their paternal grandparents.

Since Ellen was granted full custody of the children, she has complete authority over visitation. She controls the variables. If Ellen is afraid the grandparents may try to exert a negative influence, she can dictate that the visit take place in her home, in her presence.

Again, evaluate your real motives and fears. Most grandparents want something quite simple. To know and love their grandchildren. Know the difference between real and imagined negative effects.

How does your present spouse feel about contact with

people from a former marriage? Is he or she threatened by such a relationship? These are important questions. Your decisions should be based on thorough self-examination as well as your spouse's views. If your decision is contrary to your spouse's desires, communication and compromise will be vital to the relationship.

THE GOAL

Finish your self-evaluation. Wipe the sweat from your brow. Tighten the grip on your pencil, and put your goal into writing. Consider the following options to accomplish your goal:

1) *"I would like to maintain a loving relationship with my ex-laws."* It is possible. Examine your present relationship with the target people. How do they feel about you? About your children (if any)? Have you ever asked them what kind of relationship they want with you? Does your presence make them uncomfortable? Does their presence make you uncomfortable?

Don't discuss problem areas that caused the divorce with ex-laws. You don't need to tell them "your side." More often than not, both sides of a divorce are public knowledge. If they didn't see it before, they won't see it now.

2) *"I would like a close, comfortable relationship with my present in-laws."* An admirable desire. Many things can help accomplish this goal. If there are grandchildren, facilitate visitations. Make it as easy as possible for the in-laws to see your spouse and children.

Be open and honest when asked about a former marriage. Use discretion during discussions, however. It is best not to assign or assume blame. Answer the questions you are comfortable with, and politely put off others. It won't hurt anyone's feelings for you to say, "I'm sorry, but my former marriage is difficult for me to discuss."

3) *"I want my children to maintain their relationship with their grandparents. We don't have to be friends, but I don't want to be enemies, either."* This is the most common option for parents. It's realistic and obtainable. Your attitude is extremely important in establishing this type of relationship.

Resist the temptation to be defensive. If your children love their grandparents, and you help them to maintain a healthy relationship, your children will respect and love you more than ever. Even angry in-laws will find it difficult to find fault with you, if your attitude is right.

4) *"I believe any type of relationship between my former in-laws and my family is not only impossible, but harmful. I want no further contact."* Many people cannot control their bitterness and anger. They inflict their pain on others. A child should not have to endure degradation of either parent. If former relatives cannot keep derogatory remarks about *either* parent to themselves, they must ultimately be removed from the picture.

Consider and pray carefully. Don't let your own insecurities interfere with relationships that could benefit your child.

5) *"My relationship with my present in-laws is strained at best. I don't believe it will improve."* First, consider the possibility of improvement. Could they have preconceived ideas about you or your former marriage? If an opportunity arises to discuss your relationship with your in-laws, do so. Approach each visit with a they-can't-get-to-me-this-time attitude.

When all else fails, remember your spouse. If you would rather drink castor oil than visit your in-laws, strive for peace. Don't put your spouse in the middle. Even justified remarks about your in-laws will hurt your spouse. They are an important part of his or her life.

WATER BALLS

One of the first pets my husband and I owned was a duck. Nelson was a "he" until I came home one day to find that Nelson had laid an egg. By then, he was used to her name, so we still called her Nelson. Nelson was your ordinary, everyday, housebroken duck. Her favorite time of day was the afternoon when she got to go scuba diving in the bath tub.

One thing that fascinated me about her was her ability to stay dry. No matter how long Nelson bobbed in the bathtub, she never absorbed water. I guess that's why you never see a water-logged duck. I used to pour water on her back just to watch the water form balls and roll off.

When you remarry, you need to grow duck feathers. A duck's feathers are hollow, soft, and pliable so the duck can fly. Without effort, they repel water and the duck never sinks.

Even in a first marriage you find difficult people. In remarriage the number of fringe people with whom you must deal multiplies. Develop the ability to let minor irritations roll off your back or you will sink. Like a rock.

Oil yourself with these verses from Proverbs:

"A fool shows his annoyance at once, but a prudent man overlooks an insult" (Prov. 12:16).

"A gentle answer turns away wrath, but a harsh word stirs up anger" (Prov. 15:1).

"A hot-tempered man man stirs up dissension, but a patient man calms a quarrel" (Prov. 15:18).

"Starting a quarrel is like breaching a dam; so drop the matter before a dispute breaks out" (Prov. 17:14).

With a little patience, understanding, and a few duck feathers, you will form a border to your puzzle. What a puzzle! And it's not even half done yet.

TIME TO CONSIDER

1. What do you accomplish when you're angry? Do you feel better? Do you change anyone's behavior?

2. What keeps you from having positive relationships with your fringe people?

3. How can those relationships be improved?

4. What do you feel is your responsibility in your relationships with others?

6

···

Yours, Mine, and Ours

Every year, all around the country, churches plan the immortal Memorial Day picnic. At every picnic, someone jumps up and yells, "It's time for the tug-o-war competition!" Sides are chosen, ropes are produced, and people stand ready to yank and have their arms pulled from their sockets. Inevitably someone will say, "Shh. Let go of the rope."

My church had the picnic. Someone brought a rope. Teams formed, and our side had thirty women and children with two or three men thrown in "for good measure." We stood facing fifteen broad-smiling, burly beef-eaters. A side-of-beef-per-meal types. As that boisterous bevy of brawny bullies battled for the privilege of last man on the rope, I passed instructions down the line of my team. "When he says go, count to five and let go of the rope."

Would they do it?

The referee shouted, "GO!"

We hung on. ONE. The most unladylike grunts rose from behind me. TWO. Our heels dug trenches in the grass and dirt. THREE. Cheers began to ring from the other side as they watched us slowly give way to their strength. FOUR. Just a second more . . . FIVE! Like a broken rubber band, the rope snapped as we released our grip. A collective "Whoa!" sounded as fifteen hunks of muscle and over-developed bellies tumbled together. They hit the ground with a solid thunk.

A woman on our team lightly brushed her palms and with a cheerful smile said, "Oh, I guess you guys win."

YOURS AND MINE

One of a child's first words is "mine". With one little word, a baby communicates: "Hands off, buster. I had it first—get your own." Thus begins our struggle to identify and maintain our personal belongings. If someone else has the audacity to claim one of our possessions, we tighten our grip and grit our teeth. So starts the tug-o-war.

By the time a man or woman marries for the first time, they have usually brought their possessive tendencies into a sense of balance. Not always, but usually. What happens when the scales are tipped?

Both Earnest and Judy have been married before. They dated each other four years before they felt comfortable discussing marriage. Even after four years, they each brought into marriage a suitcase of war wounds and scars.

During his divorce, Earnest fought with his wife over everything. And lost. For two years, Earnest and his ex-wife insulted each other and battled over every possession. When the war ended, his former spouse had the house, the kids, the car, and the cat.

Judy never fought for anything. Her husband entered the bedroom one night, a packed suitcase in his hand. He looked straight at her and said, "Goodbye, Judy. I'm moving into an apartment. I left a little something in the bank account for you, but you'll want to find a job soon." He turned around and walked out the door.

Judy's attorney traced most of the former couple's assets, but Judy refused to take her ex-husband to court. She just let go.

For four years, Earnest and Judy lived in separate households. They made independent decisions; furnished individual homes. Can they integrate their lives, their belongings, and their bank accounts? How much should children be expected to share?

ENDLESS POSSIBILITIES

Integration is possible, but it takes time, patience, and squabbles.

My sister Cindy is three years older than I am. For most of our developing years, we shared a bedroom. Cindy was neat and tidy. Items of sentimental value held little interest for her. Wonderful things like a chicken feather from Pompa's yard were simply clutter to Cindy. To me, the feather from the adopted Indian grandfather was a link with the little Indian in me. The one who climbed trees and huge boulders. The girl who wanted to ride horses needed that feather in case she found a horse.

Since then, I've lost some of my penchant for clutter. My children found it. So did my husband. An enjoyable afternoon for my family is to go "junkin'." We find some of the weirdest things. My children love every find because they found it with Daddy. Every piece is precious.

In remarriage, two families occupy one house. Out of necessity, objects must be sorted. A practical person would tell you to be realistic. You can't keep everything. Go through all of your possessions, and what you don't absolutely need, toss. A practical person would say, "If it smells or don't do nothin', you don't want it!"

But the little clutterbug in me whispers, "There are some things precious, not practical."

Before you throw something away, be sensitive to your partner. You both need familiar objects around you. A home is a combined bin of memories. Even a few bittersweet memories.

Children especially need their favorite memorabilia around them. The old baseball glove may be worn and too small, but it's a reminder of good times. Good feelings.

Some of my best and worst memories are contained in a tattered old notebook. Doodles and nonsensical scribblings adorn the front of the notebook, but inside are my treasures. I was in the fourth grade when I wrote my first poem. My teacher read it and encouraged me to write more. I began to write down everything I felt. Some of it was happy, some of it sad.

None of what I wrote could be called glowing literature, but all of it is precious to me. That notebook is a travel diary through my life. I look back rarely. But when I need to, I go to my notebook.

My husband wouldn't see value in a beat up old notebook with scraps of paper in it. He would do the practical thing and throw it away. Sometimes it hurts to be practical.

Never toss another person's possession. If you must sort your childrens' belongings, do it in their presence. Use it as an opportunity to understand your child or stepchild better. Be on the alert for objects that hold special memories. Ask why something is special, and let them talk. You get to know others by the "junk" they keep.

THE MONEY TREE

Family assets present interesting problems for couples re-entering marital waters. People who lost great amounts of money or property in previous divorce settlements tend to be a bit shy about community property. Hence the high marketability of prenuptial agreements. We enter the hazy maze of legal aspects and maneuvers.

Most states have community property laws; when a couple marries, all property is thrown into the family well. If they sign a prenuptial agreement, the couple negotiates what property belongs to whom in the event of death or divorce. The legal variations in both of these situations are enough to make a tornado dizzy. A good lawyer may seem beyond your over-worked budget, but you will lose far more money by ignoring the need for legal advice.

Prenuptial agreements present several problems. They tend to be inflexible. A couple's financial picture is constantly in transition, and agreements must reflect change. Many prenuptial agreements are reflections of mistrust. Couples in remarriage don't come into the wedding with the high expectations they held in their first marriage. Instead, in the back of their minds, a question hangs: "What if it happens again? Then I have to start all over one more time."

God instructs us to cleave to our spouse and become one flesh. The biggest problem with a prenuptial agreement is that it nurtures division. How do you become one flesh with his and her bank accounts? "Your money" and "my money" arguments develop over who pays "our rent" and buys "our groceries." People who want everything neatly divided into two piles usually think they're being short-changed in some way.

Assets must be shared and financial decisions made

61

jointly. Anything less and you are holding back from each other.

Many remarried couples face the problem with a wry grin. Anna told me, "Sure we share everything. I share the child support I never get, and he shares the salary that doesn't go far enough to support two households. We both get half of nothing."

Money is usually tight for the remarried couple. Families are large, and two or more households are maintained. Legal bills sit on the corner of a desk and scream, *"Pay me!"* Both people work to provide for their family.

It is important that a father pay child support for his children. His responsibility began with the child's birth and is not affected by divorce or distance. A child has difficulty believing in the father's love when the father will not provide basic support.

The new wife may nod her head in agreement about child support, but inside her bones ache with resentment. Her own children have needs, and sometimes it seems priority is given to the "other" family.

While it is difficult to draw a straight line between the needs of one family and another, a compromise must be reached. Be objective. Be fair. Ideally, all the parents must be involved in the financial decisions concerning children. A stepparent's responsibility to the acquired family is as real and important as the responsibility to a biological family. It takes a carefully balanced scale on a tight budget to be fair with both. But fair you must be.

IDEALS

The circle winds around, and once again we face ideals. In ideal remarriage, the husband has an ideal job, receives ideal pay, and is able to pay child support and provide for his ideal acquired family. In "ideal" remarriage, children share generously with weekend siblings. They say to each other, "Here! Sleep in my room. I was lonely anyway," or "Please! You use the bathroom first, I've used it first lots of times."

Ideals. What if our lives are less than ideal? What can I do when money vanishes like vapor, the kids re-enact Rambo movies, and I resent everyone in my house?

WAIT

Often only one partner believes there's a problem, or only one is interested in solutions. You can't do anything about a person who is not willing to work on marriage or family relationships. So what do you do? Leave? Stay? Cry? Laugh?

Maybe all of the above. No one can answer that question for you. But there is hope, if you just hang on.

Quit hitting your head against the wall, stand back, and watch. When you get to the place in your life when you say, "OK, Lord, I give up. I can't do anything," his power can take over.

One of my favorite Bible stories is about a servant girl named Hagar. Sarah gave Hagar to Abraham for the purpose of bearing a son. Later, after Hagar's son Ishmael was born, Sarah was jealous and forced Abraham to send the young mother and infant away. Abraham handed Hagar a skin of water, some food, and sent her and her son into the desert.

The water and food ran out. The sun burned into the mother and child until they couldn't go another step. Hagar put her baby under one of the bushes. Then she went off and sat down nearby, for she thought, "I cannot watch the boy die." As she sat there, she began to sob (Gen. 21:8-20, paraphrased).

An angel came to Hagar. He spoke to her and opened her

eyes to a well of water. The Lord heard her cry and responded.

God could have prevented Abraham from sending Hagar to the desert. Or he could have shown her the well before she ran out of water. But he waited. He waited for her to sit down and give up.

Sometimes we must give up. Sit down. Wait.

King David understood human futility. In the middle of his frustration and anguish, he wrote many psalms. Psalm 40 is a record of how God answered David. And how he answers us:

> I waited patiently for the Lord;
> He turned to me and heard my cry.
> He lifted me out of the slimy pit,
> out of the mud and mire;
> He set my feet on a rock
> and gave me a firm place to stand.
> He put a new song in my mouth,
> a hymn of praise to our God.
> Many will see and fear
> and put their trust in the Lord
> (Ps. 40:1-3).

Right now it may seem as if you will never get through all your problems. But change is a constant. In a year from today, you may look back at the problems you face now and say, "Whew! We made it! I never thought we could, but God brought us through it."

Five years from now you may even say, "What was I so worried about?"

TIME TO CONSIDER

As a mother, I understand the helpless agony Hagar felt as she surrendered her son under a bush. She had done all she could do; nothing was left but death. She sobbed. Her sobs reached beyond the desert and caught the ear of God. But before the Lord met Hagar, she had to release her hold. She couldn't hold onto her son or herself any longer. If Hagar had kept a tenacious hold on the rope of self reliance, she would have lost the tug-o-war. She won by letting go.

God restored life to Hagar and gave a promise to her and the boy under the bush.

1. What are you holding onto? Material possessions? Children? Pride? What do these things do for your marriage?

2. What objects or possessions seem most valuable to your partner? To you? Why?

3. Who makes the financial decisions in your family? Are finances a source of friction for you? Why?

4. Describe the biggest wall you have encountered in your present marriage to date. Did you get past it? If so, how? If not, why not?

5. Can you see any walls in the distance? Describe them.

6. When do you give up and hand a situation over to God?

7. What is usually the result when you try to resolve problems on your own? What is the result when you give them to the Lord? Why is there a difference?

7
…
Holidays!

It was midnight. Darkness smothered the house, and still air carried no whispers of sound. Stranger leaned back in his chair and stretched. His neck muscles stiffened and his eyes burned. The old man worked silently and quickly beside Stranger.

With a vigorous shake of his head, Stranger tried to dispel his lethargy. But he was tired. He was weary in bone, sinew, and soul.

"Can we not leave it and continue in the morning?" he quietly asked.

"No." The old man's answer was soft but without waver.

A small bubble of resentment burst in the pit of Stranger's stomach and rose as bile in his throat. "But why?! What is the purpose? I have been with you all this time, and still you won't tell me the purpose!"

The old man said nothing.

In agitation, Stranger rose from his chair and crossed the room to the window. He felt childish for his outburst, but he felt anger for the still silence. Slowly he turned to face the old man again. "Will I ever know why I came here?"

The old man stopped his work, laid down the scissors, and looked at Stranger. "What you really ask of me is to confirm what you already know. I could tell you now why I work the puzzles. You don't understand my methods, and you question them. If I explained my ways to you now, you would try to change them. I know what the picture will look like. Do you?"

Stranger shook his head. "No. How could I know?"

"You can't. My knowledge makes my hands sure and my methods right. I believe you want to see the picture finished and whole. Will you stay with me?"

The old man's calm spirit washed away some of the fear and anger that had settled on Stranger's heart. Once again, he took a chair at the table and set his mind to seek out missing puzzle pieces. Yes, the work was tedious. But it must be done.

THE FAMILY TENNIS MATCH

Something strange happens when you're a spectator at a tennis match. As you sit on the sidelines, your eyes pursue the ball back and forth across the net. With each pass, your head turns to follow the all important orb. Left. Right. Left. Right. With each turn of your head, a little clicker counts the volleys. Left, click. Right, click. And so on. By the end of a volley, your clicker sums up; you turn to the person next to you and say, "Wow! That was 468 shots!"

Jigsaw families participate in holiday tennis tournaments, using children as the tennis balls. A spectator can grow dizzy watching a child fly over the net, only to be smacked right back again. The clickers keep counting.

Divorced and restructured families spend holidays bouncing around to please other people. Children are shuffled forward and back on days when they long to be home playing with new toys or visiting friends. And for every child off to visit, a parent is left behind with a hollow house and heart.

One step beyond the lonely parent and the ricochet child is the stepparent and parent who must diplomatically create and maintain a festive holiday atmosphere. A difficult task. So difficult, in fact, some parents give up their holiday visitation rights.

In all the hurry and commotion, it's easy to get trapped on a treadmill. The ground under our feet keeps spinning around and around, ever faster. We either keep up with the treadmill or get swept under.

One of the most famous New Testament stories is the one where Jesus fed five thousand people with five loaves of bread and two fish. Mark 6 gives a short preface to the mass banquet.

Jesus had sent out the apostles to preach repentance and perform miracles. When they returned to Jesus, they reported to Him all they had done and taught. "Then, because so many people were coming and going that they did not even have a chance to eat, he said to them, 'Come with me by yourselves to a quiet place and get some rest.' So they went away by themselves in a boat to a solitary place" (Mark 6:31,32).

When you are on the treadmill, do you hear him say it? "Come with me by yourself to a quiet place and get some rest."

Can you accept the invitation?

69

LOGISTICS

The first problem that crops up before a holiday is physical logistics, such as how to transport children to the place they should be at the right time. Whether they want to be there or not.

One family experienced complications at Easter: "Ed and I argued for half an hour over the phone about transportation," Shelly told me. "He felt it was my responsibility to deliver the kids to his house; I felt he should pick them up. I got tired of arguing so I said I'd bring them over at 3:00. He said no, he wouldn't be home till five. I changed a dentist appointment to suit his schedule. When I told my kids they were going to their father's house for Easter, they didn't want to go. I had to make them go or he'd say I stopped them. My kids went away mad at me, and I sat home alone on Easter."

Arguments about transportation can go on forever. You have two choices: 1) Fight for the next ten years, or 2) provide the transportation. If you decide to provide transportation, do it out of love for your children. Not martyrdom.

SARDINES

Okay, the children arrive. Fantastic! They're finally here! Now, where do you put them?

The youth group in our church loves to play a game called sardines. It's a twist on hide and seek, and it's great for bringing a group close together. Literally. To play it, everyone gathers in one room. We usually turn off every light in the church to add difficulty. We choose one person to hide and everyone else stays in the "safe" room until the one hiding has enough time to find a secret place. Then everyone spreads out on their own and seeks.

The twist to this game comes when you find the one hiding. You don't turn him in. You hide with him. Each person eventually finds the hiding place and squishes in until only one person is left. That person is "it" and hides the next time around. If you don't like people or body odor, don't play this game.

Jigsaw families may find themselves involuntary players in a game of sardines when family members combine for holidays. If you live in a house built for four or five people and three or more come to visit, things become cramped. Privacy and quiet are luxuries, and bathrooms . . . there are never enough bathrooms.

Shelly married Don, who has custody of his two daughters. Shelly has four girls of her own, none of whom live with them. Shelly and Don bought a three bedroom house with one bathroom. It was just right. Most of the time. Last Christmas, Shelly's four daughters spent a week with Don and Shelly. That's seven females and one male with one bathroom.

By noon the first day, Shelly knew they had a problem.

A solution appeared when she told a friend, "It's like playing musical chairs with a bathroom."

Shelly set a portable tape player on the bathroom counter, put in a music tape, and explained the rules to the family. "When you go into the bathroom, turn on the tape player. When two songs have played, get out. It's the next person's turn."

Shelly's solution would not work in every situation, but it worked for her family. The key ingredients were action and cooperation. When a situation becomes uncomfortable, the worst thing to do is ignore it and mark the days on the calendar until life returns to normal. Shelly and Don did not build four more bathrooms to make their daughters more comfortable. They developed a system that would motivate everyone to be more cooperative. Cooperation makes potentially unpleasant conditions not only bearable, but enjoyable.

Charice found other ways to make crowded visitations pleasant for the entire family. She and her husband live in a three bedroom duplex. On many holidays, seven children descend upon their home. The children I interviewed said holidays are relaxed and enjoyable.

"One thing we did from the start," Charice explained, "was to keep sleeping bags, pillows, pajamas, and tooth-brushes handy for all the kids. They're always in the same place, and the kids feel at home." She laughed a little. "It gets noisy, but we try to laugh. After the first year, the kids acted like it was a big slumber party. They love it!"

If you keep a few of their own toys, books, or games on hand, it helps develop a sense of family membership as opposed to visitor.

GUILT

A child with divorced parents is pulled apart emotionally because of loyalty. Even a child physically abused by one or more parents feels deep loyalty to both his mother and father. He often feels as though he has abandoned the parent with whom he doesn't live. Conversely, he feels guilty if he enjoys visiting the non-custodial parent. It's not uncommon for a child to sabotage a visit or holiday in order to relieve guilt. "If I have a terrible time at Dad's, Mom won't feel hurt."

Custody battles are not new. King Solomon was called on to settle a custody dispute. Two prostitutes came before him with a baby boy, and each claimed the child as her son. Solomon gave an order. "Cut the living child in two and give half to one and half to the other" (1 Kings 3:25).

The real mother said "Please my lord, give her the living

baby! Don't kill him!"

The impostor said, "Neither I nor you shall have him. Cut him in two!" (v.26).

The mother loved her child enough to let him go rather than watch him be cut in two. The woman who grieved the death of her own child wanted her pain inflicted on someone else.

Children of divorced parents are often ripped in two by parents who see only their own pain. Guilt is a mighty sword, and it threatens the emotional life of your child. Can you see through your wounded eyes well enough to ease away the sword?

A child's guilt is best dealt with by both parents. Parents can give their children a tremendous gift of freedom with these words: "I love you. Your mother (father) loves you. When you are with her (him), I want you to enjoy yourself. I'm glad you love your mom (dad), and I know it doesn't affect how you feel about me."

The words are simple, easy to understand, and best of all, they release a pressure valve. They may even heal some of your own hurt.

After the words are said, you must reinforce the message. Voice and facial expressions can contradict what the mouth utters.

1) Convince yourself before you convince your child. What you are giving your child, freedom from guilt, is a gift. It is natural and good for children to love their parents, even when the parents no longer love each other.

2) Let your children describe their visits. A normal response after a day of fun is to tell someone about it. If you are the one your child wants to tell, take it as a compliment. Throw in a "that's great!" here and there.

Parents also suffer from guilt. Fear sits on their shoulders. At opportune moments it whispers in their ears, "It's your fault the kid's in trouble. You destabilized his home."

Divorce and remarriage do affect children. At times severely. It wouldn't be honest to say otherwise. But there comes an age when children must take responsibility for their own actions. The longer excuses are made for poor behavior, the easier it is for the behavior to continue. It's a trap that catches the parent and child and destroys them both.

TRADITIONS

There is satisfaction in the yearly reminders of family continuity represented by traditions. When a tradition must be broken for one reason or another, the family members suffer loss. Ironically, some traditions are reminders of a painful past.

Erin and Phillip shared a wonderful first Christmas with Erin's sons and Phillip's daughter. At the beginning of the season, the family sat down together to plan their holiday. They cooked popcorn and played Christmas music on the stereo. Then they discussed favorite holiday traditions. They all had at least one tradition that was special to them. Tasks such as cookie baking and decorating were divided so everyone had an equal part in the creation of celebration.

Phillip's daughter explained how the early planning helped her adjust to the new family situation: "It was really neat. I don't live with Dad and Erin, but this way I felt included. I didn't just come over to their house on Christmas morning and open presents. We started some new traditions. I felt close to my dad again."

LEFT BEHIND

As the parent who must endure a holiday without your children, you hurt. Feelings of rejection, fear, loneliness, and anger are common.

A friend described her first holiday alone: "I missed my kids so much I thought the pain would kill me. I went through old photo albums and thought about our holidays before the divorce. I loved to watch them open presents or find eggs. When they were gone, I even began to miss their father. There was a time when we were happy as a family. I remember the love and the fun we had. I miss all of it, and I'll never have it back."

The only way I could empathize with my friend was to think back to the emotional aftermath of my son's death. I ached and cried and went through photos. I mourned the loss of my son and the loss of motherhood. For a time, I believed I could never be whole again.

In a sense, both my hurting friend and I were right. You can't go back. Life will never be the same. The Lord has assigned us a time to grieve for what we have lost. "There is a time for everything, and a season for every activity under heaven . . . a time to weep and a time to laugh, a time to mourn and a time to dance" (Eccles. 3:1,4).

LIFE AT NINETY MILES PER HOUR

Think back to last Christmas. On December 26th, did you look in the mirror and see a person with hair blown straight back? Were your lips forced into a desperate grin? Did you find kamikaze bugs stuck to your glasses?

It was a holiday in the fast lane. But you survived. You will again. With effort, each holiday can be better. Slower paced. Your children will adjust, your new spouse will become more at ease, and the old spouse may even cooperate.

During the most difficult times of my life, an echo sounded in my mind. *This too shall pass.* It will pass for you too. You may have lost much of your hair by then, but it will pass.

75

TIME TO CONSIDER

Before you consider the following questions, think about the message Jesus sent specifically to you:

I have told you these things, so that in me you may have peace. In this world you will have trouble. But take heart! I have overcome the world (John 16:33).

Come with me by yourselves to a quiet place and get some rest (Mark 6:31).

1. CUSTODIAL PARENT: What makes you grind your teeth when your children visit the other parent? Why does it hurt? (It's okay if it doesn't hurt. You may be thankful for a free weekend or evening.)

NON-CUSTODIAL PARENT: How do you feel when your children are scheduled for a visit?

2. CUSTODIAL PARENT: Do you secretly hope your children will have a terrible time with the other parent? If so, why?

NON-CUSTODIAL PARENT: Do you make visits a "Disneyland" experience? How do you react to a child who is less than enthusiastic about seeing you?

3. Draw or picture a circle in your mind. This circle represents the family as a unit. Make a dot or mark for each family member somewhere in, on, or around the circle. Then explain the position of each mark. Who represented the mark most difficult to place? Why?

4. What would be the "ideal" holiday picture for your entire family? Could it ever be reality? Why or why not?

5. When Jesus offered rest to the disciples, there was a prerequisite. "*Come with me by yourselves* to a quiet place. . . ." How can you spend a little extra time alone with Jesus?

8

...

Comparison Shopping

"Man, Sarah!" Dennis exclaimed in exasperation. "Why can't you be more like Michelle? She's so calm and relaxed about everything."

Dennis' comment floored me. It wasn't false modesty that made my mouth drop open, my eyes bug out, and my raspy voice say, "Huh?!"

Let's get some perspective on Dennis' wish. His wife, Sarah, is June Cleaver, Julia Childs, and Miss America all rolled into one tidy five foot, two inch, 105 pound package. She's organized, crafty, and a great cook. Sarah doesn't just sew, she designs her own patterns.

Dennis was comparing Sarah to me! The girl in high school home economics who put red food coloring into a banana cream pie instead of vanilla. It tasted even worse than it looked. The girl who finds strange things in her refrigerator—like a book. I use a sewing machine to mend and repair. Create? Hah! Dennis wanted his wife to be more like me?

Dennis appreciates the admirable qualities in his wife. His comparison had to do with my relaxed nature and Sarah's nervous energy. But his comment hurt and embarrassed Sarah and made me uncomfortable. Like many of us, Dennis wants the perfect mate. His idea of the perfect wife was most of Sarah and a little of me.

PEOPLE BUILDERS

Have you seen toy plastic building blocks that snap together? Wouldn't it be nice if people were made out of similar blocks? When we wanted a husband, a wife, or even children, we could build them the way we wanted. If I liked something about one person, I could take a block from him and put it with a personality trait I admired in someone else. I'd get rid of the blocks I didn't like, and when everything was put together, a perfect person would stand ready to sweep me off my feet.

The problem is a perfect person could not live with me. He would go out of his mind. Unless he tried to rebuild me, and I don't want someone messing with my blocks.

When Dennis compared me to Sarah, my mind immediately ran its own comparison test. A knot of envy tied itself around me. I wish I could be just like Sarah. Or so I thought.

I retracted my wish after I had time to think it over. All the good qualities I have are a package deal with the poor qualities. They make up my whole person. The relaxed nature Dennis admired could not tackle all the projects and activities that Sarah's nervous energy handles with apparent ease. Sarah would not have the patience to spend several hundred hours writing with the hope a book would emerge.

THE SECRET PLACES

If human intellect were responsible for the design of the female reproductive system, babies would form in a resealable pouch instead of an enclosed womb. The pouch would be transparent. As the baby developed, we could reach in and make alterations to suit us.

I'm so glad God didn't leave it up to us. I agree with David: "Such knowledge is too wonderful for me, too lofty for me to attain" (Ps. 139:6).

"For you created my inmost being; you knit me together in my mother's womb. I praise you because I am fearfully and wonderfully made; your works are wonderful, I know that full well. My frame was not hidden from you when I was made in the secret place. When I was woven together in the depths of the earth, your eyes saw my unformed body" (Ps. 139:13-15).

The Lord creates us as a whole being. Physical, mental, emotional, and spiritual beings. He didn't build an empty shell. He filled it with intellect and eccentricities. He knows what's inside of us.

Somewhere I saw a sign that said, "A friend is someone who knows everything about you . . . and loves you anyway."

Jesus is such a friend because he is with us from the beginning. He knows our habits, our failures, our joys, our pain, even our anger. And he loves us anyway. He accepts us.

We all need acceptance from our mate. Comparisons reject acceptance. We make comparisons because we want to rebuild another person. Even when we mean the comparison as a compliment, it is a destructive habit.

When Cheryl met her second husband Pete she was immediately attracted to him. He was everything her first husband was not. Her first husband was tall, dark-haired, and rough in voice and action. Pete was also tall, but blond, and very gentle. His voice was smooth and even. Never impulsive, Pete liked to think twice about every move he made.

During their courtship, Cheryl used comparisons as a compliment. "I'm so glad you're not like my first husband. He spent money so fast we never had any to pay bills." Or, "You're so sweet and patient. Stan was such a hot head."

At first, Pete's ego was bolstered because Cheryl obviously preferred him to her former husband. After Cheryl and Pete were married, however, Pete began to withdraw. He talked to Cheryl less and less. Cheryl felt the tremors of their tottering relationship but couldn't understand the cause. One day, out of hurt and anger, Cheryl erupted. She said the first words that came to mind. "At least with Stan I always knew where I stood!"

Pete looked briefly at Cheryl. He shook his head slightly, and said, "Maybe you'd better go back to Stan." He turned on his heel and walked out the door.

Pete and Cheryl eventually agreed to see a counselor. Cheryl began to understand how comparing Pete's good qualities to Stan's poor attributes made Pete withdraw. When Cheryl continually compared the two men on surface issues, Pete wondered whether she made other comparisons as well. His sexual desires were hampered by fear of competition. Decisions about his stepchildren were difficult because he wondered what Stan would do. Pete often felt Cheryl used comparisons to manipulate his behavior. The comparisons became a warning signal. "If you do this, you'll be just like Stan."

Through counseling, both Pete and Cheryl learned to verbalize their feelings and fears in acceptable ways.

ACCEPTANCE

How do we learn to accept someone without reservation or comparison? Look at the person as a whole. The way God made him or her, not the way you would like that person to be.

If you read the Bible from Genesis to Revelation, you will find only one perfect being. God. There is not one human being who could claim perfection. Time after time, man has let God down. From Adam to you and I, man has always made mistakes. Yet the Lord has never stopped loving us. He loves us as we are. With every fault.

Jesus knew Peter. Simon Peter was brash, headstrong, and impulsive. But he loved the Lord. When Jesus told the disciples he was leaving, Peter asked, "Lord, why can't I follow you now? I will lay down my life for you."

Then Jesus answered, "Will you really lay down your life for me? I tell you the truth, before the rooster crows, you will disown me three times!" (John 13:37,38).

Peter did deny Jesus three times. Afterwards, Luke tells us Peter went outside and wept bitterly. I believe Peter wept because he let the Lord down, and worse, Jesus knew he would. But the story doesn't end there.

After the resurrection, Jesus found Simon Peter and a few other disciples back in their old fishing boat. He asked them to have breakfast with him on the shore by the Sea of Tiberias. There Jesus asked Peter, "Simon son of John, do you truly love me more than these?"

"Yes, Lord," he said, "you know that I love you" (John 21:15).

Jesus could have said, "Then where were you when I needed you? You denied knowing me!"

But he didn't. Jesus said, "Feed my lambs."

Peter was reinstated with Christ. He was not accused for

83

his failures. He was accepted.

The kind of love and acceptance Jesus gave Peter built him up. It didn't tear him down. Jesus' love gave Peter strength. What kind of love do you give?

Stop the comparison cycle. Put on rose colored glasses now and then, and ignore the faults in your spouse. Build up the person you married.

One woman told me, "I know why my husband fell for his girlfriend. She's always telling him he's good at this or great at that. He'd probably still love me if I said stuff like that. But I just can't. I don't feel like it."

There is only one question for this woman. "How difficult is it to pay someone a compliment?" She wouldn't have to lie or flatter. An hour earlier she told me her ex-husband was a great father. Yet she couldn't tell him. Pride and fear of rejection kept her silent.

GREENER GRASS

Jeff is single now, but he has been married three times. He summed up his divorces with one sentence. "I was always looking for greener grass."

Unfortunately for Jeff and the three women he married, the grass *was* green in each succeeding marriage. But until he lived in it he didn't realize it was crab grass.

TIME TO CONSIDER

When you think about it, Peter didn't deserve Jesus' love and faith. Neither do we. We all fail him. We fail each other. Your former partner failed you. Your present spouse will disappoint you at times. But when you make comparisons, everyone loses, including you.

1. What causes people to make comparisons? Do you feel as though you are being compared to someone else?

2. Do past memories interfere with present relationships?

3. Which qualities in your present spouse do you admire? Which qualities irritate you?

4. Which qualities do you tend to notice the most? Why?

5. Do you feel like you must compete with a former spouse? Why?

6. What changes must be made in a person's personality or habits to be accepted by Christ? What changes do you want other people to make before you can accept them? Do you expect more than Jesus?

7. Think about the best friend you've ever had (excluding Jesus). Why are you friends? What did you do to deserve the friendship? Why do you care so much about that person?

8. How can you use the answers to question 7 to affect your marriage?

9. How do you know the Lord loves and accepts you as you are? How do the people around you know you love and accept them?

9
...

If Only We Could Leave This Chapter Out

Stranger placed another piece into the addled picture. He couldn't rid himself of the vague discomfort. With every shape he positioned in the puzzle, he felt a fingernail of apprehension run down his spine. At first, the sensation was hardly a tickle. But as time passed beyond the highest hour, and the puzzle formed pictures nearly recognizable, the pressure increased. It hurt.

For a reason he could not name, Stranger had to work faster. He knew the old man watched him, but neither of them spoke. Where was that piece?

Stranger's agitation grew. It stretched him. Hurt him. Ah! Another piece! But where was the blue one?

The old man quit working. Stranger never noticed. There was something wrong. What was it?

The fingernail scraped, and Stranger's back arched to

escape. His fists clenched and flexed. "What is it?!" Stranger's voice beat hollow echoes against stone walls.

Still, the old man watched. Stranger's eyes returned to the puzzle. This time they did not seek. They saw. As he looked at the unfinished picture, a knife plunged through his chest, and his mind imploded with acrid anguish.

"No." His dry throat squeezed and gargled until the word escaped again with physical force, "NO!" He came to his feet as he tipped the table and threw it smashing across the room. The puzzle pieces scattered like bird seed on the floor.

"It's mine!" he foamed through gritted teeth. He turned to where the old man still sat. "It's mine! And you knew. I threw it away, and you dug it all out again! Can't you see what it's done to me? Talk to me! How dare you do this to me?"

The old man placed his hands on his knees. He said nothing.

"You were so full of wisdom earlier! Where is it now?" Stranger mocked. "I'm leaving, old man. I. . . ." Stranger stopped. He whirled. The room had no door. But that's impossible. Two windows but no door. He ran to the wall and beat it with his fists. He kicked. In fury he cast his body against the wall of rocks until, battered, he sank to the floor. His self-inflicted torture shaded consciousness. Stranger's bruised hands clutched his knees, and he lay curled in a hollow ball.

Writing has always been a friend and a comfort for me. But this chapter has been different. The preparation, the interviews, and the memories have etched permanent autographs on my heart. I would rather leave this chapter out of the book. But I can't. Since some of the people involved in a jigsaw family are not blood relatives, the taboo of incest may be less intimidating. To ignore the frightening possibility of sexual exploitation is to ignore the misery of the victims. A support book for jigsaw families is incomplete without a chapter on this painful subject.

If you have been sexually molested, currently or in the past, this chapter won't even begin to address your needs. You need intimate help and prayer. If you've never told anyone about the molestation, I urge you to do three things:

1) *Pray and read the Bible.* Sexual abuse kills something deep inside. It turns the heart to stone, then rolls the stone over the soul like a rock in front of a sepulcher. But listen. Jesus stands just outside the sepulcher, and he weeps. Before Jesus raised Lazarus from the dead, his spirit was troubled, and he wept (see John 11:33-35). Prior to the crucifixion, Jesus prayed in Gethsemane. He began to be sorrowful and troubled. Then he said to his disciples, "My soul is overwhelmed with sorrow to the point of death. Stay here and keep watch with me" (Matt. 26:37,38).

In each situation, Jesus knew the outcome. But he still felt the pain. He wept with Mary and Martha, the sisters of Lazarus, because their moment of grief was poignant. In Gethsemane he faced his own pain and grief as well as his friends'.

Now he feels all your hurt, anger, and sorrow. He knows your future and what he can do for you, but he doesn't minimize your feelings right now.

2) *Find someone you trust and confide in him.* I once had a small cut that became infected. It was red and swollen with a thin red streak that began at the wound and ran up my arm. The red streak was blood poisoning. As treatment, the doctor took a firm hold on my wrist and reopened the cut. He vigorously scrubbed the infected area while a nurse poured a disinfectant onto the cut that made my whole arm feel like fire. As a reflex, I tried to yank my arm

away from the doctor's grasp, but he held me tight. Finally, a bandage was put on my wound to prevent further infection.

Incest victims are walking, talking, infected wounds. The cuts are neglected until red streaks begin to show. It's agony to reopen and scrub a wound, but it must be done to heal.

You need a friend, a pastor, or a counselor who will hold you tight until your wound can be cleansed, disinfected, and bandaged. It takes someone special.

As Jesus hung on the cross, he looked down and saw his mother and "the disciple whom he loved" standing nearby. The shredded nerves and emotions of a mother who watches her son die were etched upon Mary's face. "He said to his mother, 'Dear woman, here is your son,' and to the disciple, 'Here is your mother.' From that time on, this disciple took her into his home" (John 19:26,27).

Even with nails in his hands and feet, and with lungs screaming for air, Jesus recognized the need in his mother and friend for emotional support and comfort. He not only encouraged it, he provided it by bringing the right people together.

It may be difficult for you to believe at times, but Jesus is concerned that you receive love, support, and comfort. He will provide you with someone to listen. Best of all, he always listens.

3) *Get past your feelings of shame and guilt.* Satan uses guilt to keep you from discovering God's love and acceptance. If he can make you believe that you are too dirty for Jesus, he controls your life.

Misplaced guilt is one of Satan's favorite tools. He'll never make you feel guilty over the real issues of sin in your life. He revels in the subtle sabotage of your mind and soul through the use of false accusations.

You can know the difference between Satan's accusations and God's conviction of sin. When God points out sin, we can accept responsibility and ask for forgiveness. God's mercy brings peace.

Satan hops around in circles so that his voice comes from everywhere. "See? See what you did? What a dirtbag! If people only knew...."

Can you tell the difference between Satan's snide remarks and Jesus' reassurance?

"Let us draw near to God with a sincere heart in full assurance of faith, having our hearts sprinkled to cleanse us from a guilty conscience and having our bodies washed with pure water" (Heb. 10:22).

PREVENTION

The definition of incest differs from book to book and state to state. To understand why a chapter on incest is included in this book, it might help to paraphrase the general opinion of what constitutes incest. It is a sexual act or a series of acts between members of the same family, or substitutes for family relationships. These sexual acts vary from voluntary exhibitionism to intercourse.

Family substitutes, such as step relations, are included in the definition because they hold a position of trust.

According to Dr. Chuck James, of Sumner Church of the Nazarene, the opportunities and temptations for incest can be controlled to a certain extent. Basic rules of conduct and dress should be incorporated by all families. These rules should not be instituted out of mistrust, but rather as an attempt to avoid detrimental experiences.

Dr. James suggests a first step in prevention of incest in the step-family is to discuss the need for privacy with adolescent and teenage children:

Parents should explain the relationship between "mom and dad" which brings the two families together to live in the same house. Discuss the normal adolescent and teenage curiosity and desires which represent potential problems when privacy and modesty are not respected. Listen with love to what the child says to you in the discussion. As a part of the discussion, lay ground rules for the whole family to follow.[1]

ROOF RULES

The Old Testament lists hundreds of rules. Our human nature either ignores or rebels against lists of rules. But God's laws are based on common sense and the desire to protect us from foolish acts. In Deuteronomy, a book of laws, a verse caught my eye. It said: "When you build a new house, make a parapet around your roof so that you may not bring the guilt of bloodshed on your house if someone falls from the roof" (Deut. 22:8).

At first glance, I had to smile. I filed the verse with the lists of "begats" under "Odd or Obscure Verses". But slowly, understanding fought its way into my brain. As parents, we must build parapets around our family. The parapet will keep someone from accidentally falling. If we don't want our spouse or children to fall into sin, we can take steps in the effort to keep them safe.

Note the wording of the old law. It does not say, "If you build a parapet around your house, no one will fall from your roof."

What the verse says, in Cresse paraphrase, is: "Build the parapet. Do your best to make your house safe. It is your responsibility. But you are not responsible if someone decides to jump."

A number of simple "roof rules" offer protection for

families. Dr. James offers suggestions for a list of household rules.[2] As your family discusses conduct and behavior in the home, you may come up with a few of your own.

1) *A dress code* — Every family has different ideas about modesty and style. But basics are basics. No one should run around the house in a state of undress. It takes only a moment to throw on a bathrobe for a run down the hall. This rule often means drastic changes in household habits.

2) *Knock on wood* — If a door is closed, knock, then wait for permission to enter. This rule is as important for parents to observe as the children. Parents teach respect for other people's privacy by allowing children a sense of privacy.

3) *Locks* — There are times when parents need the assurance that they will not be disturbed. A lock on the bedroom door may offer such assurance.

4) *Cognizance* — Be aware of the attitudes and emotions in your home. Ask the Lord to give you courage and wisdom when inappropriate behavior first occurs. Incest rarely occurs instantly. It's the result of culminating factors and behaviors.

5) *Sibling relationships* — Keep in mind that adolescents and teens probably won't see each other as "sisters and brothers." It's quite common for step-siblings to develop crushes on one another. It won't always lead to sexual experimentation, but opportunity adds to risk. Set rules for bedroom visits, such as open doors and off-limits hours.

Most crushes between step-siblings are innocent and taken care of in time. But there is still a need for open communication between parent and child. It can be a confusing and painful experience.

6) *Parents* — Nudity embarrasses the preadolescent or

teenage child. At this age, kids are afraid of their own physical and emotional reactions, and they often lose trust in the parent. Modesty is the best policy.

TIME TO CONSIDER

Children need and enjoy physical affection. It is essential to emotional development. Withholding affection is as harmful as abusing it. Hugs and kisses say, "You're important to me. I want you to know it."

A difference exists between honest parental or familial love and satisfaction of selfish desires. Adults are responsible to recognize one and protect from the other. It is our parapet to build.

The Lord didn't say that a parapet is easy or quick to build. Only that we are to build one.

1. How can we prevent sexual exploitation in the home?

2. Have you ever had occasion to suspect someone in your household of incest? If so, what was your reaction?

3. How can victims of incest live with memories and experience healing?

4. What kinds of feelings do you experience in a discussion on incest?

5. What do you think God's attitude is toward sexual abusers? What would you like his attitude to be?

6. What kind of "parapet" have you built around your house?

7. Write two short letters. The first should start with:

Dear Victim,

Start the second letter with:

Dear Abuser,

If you have been either a perpetrator or a victim, write a letter to yourself using the words you would like someone to say to you. Be honest and open when you write your letters. No one will see them unless you want them to. The purpose of the letters is to reveal your gut-level responses to a problem that should not exist, but does.

10

. . .

The Over-Stuffed Circle

I was in my bedroom thinking and praying, feeling a little sorry for myself. Our first son would have celebrated his seventh birthday today. A friend of mine has a seven-year-old boy, and I wondered what Jason, my son, would have been like. As I knelt beside my bed, my four-year-old son entered the room. He stood quietly and watched me. Then he stepped beside me, placed one hand on each side of my face, and said, "Mommy, I know you worked hard. Is that sweat, or are you crying?"

The day-to-day stress and struggle in jigsaw family life forces you to work hard. It's not easy, sometimes, to know the difference between sweat and tears. Often there is a mingling of both.

WRESTLING WITH THE WIND

In the whirlwind of confusion and problems, you need a stabilizer. Without an anchor, you and your family will be carried away with the leaves and branches. Your strength is not enough to wrestle with wind. You can't keep your family on the ground with human strength.

Among the twelve disciples Jesus chose, at least four were professional fishermen. Young and strong, they were accustomed to boats and unpredictable seas. One day Jesus wanted to go to the other side of the lake. They climbed into a boat and set sail.

As they sailed, he (Jesus) fell asleep. A squall came down on the lake, so that the boat was being swamped, and they were in great danger.

The disciples went and woke him, saying, "Master, Master, we're going to drown!"

He got up and rebuked the wind and the raging waters; the storm subsided and all was calm. "Where is your faith?" he asked his disciples (Luke 8:23-25).

Jesus' disciples had spent many years at sea. Their fathers had acquired much knowledge about fishing and passed it on to them; it helped them survive. Their backs and arms were sinewy and strong, and they did their best to control the boat during the storm. But the storm and waves tossed them around like toys. All their knowledge and all their strength meant nothing in the tempest. They needed Jesus.

A HOLY PASSENGER

Jigsaw family life is tempestuous. You might get along on your own for a while. But eventually, you will face a storm so fierce that your strength will give out, and your knowledge will be useless. You need Jesus in your boat. Have you brought him along?

Draw a large circle on a piece of paper. There is no need for perfection because this circle represents your life. If your life is perfect, get a drawing tool and make a perfect circle. Otherwise, just draw it by hand.

Remember, this circle represents you personally. Not your family. Not your marriage. It is you. Make a square or a dot in the center of the circle. This mark represents Christ. Make a mark for your spouse halfway between Jesus' mark and the edge of the circle. Place marks for each of your children on the inside edge of the circle. Finally, place a dot outside the circle for each situation or problem you face right now; anything from finances to problem skin.

What you have created on paper is an ideal. It is the visible evidence of God's ideal marriage.

Look at the circle. When Jesus is placed in the center of your life, you drive an anchor into the ground. Everything else you have: spouse, children, money, possessions, *everything*, can and may be taken away from you. Instantly.

Several years ago, I read about a girl who survived a tremendous flood. In a matter of minutes, she lost her family, her home, her friends. Caught in a torrent of rapid waters, her clothes were stripped away. Nothing was left, not even pride or modesty.

This battered girl had one thing that neither flood nor man could take away. Rooted at the center of her life was Jesus Christ. Through his strength alone, she survived her sorrow.

If Jesus is the center of your life, you can survive anything. If your spouse, children, or possessions are in the center of your circle, the circle disintegrates.

A friend who was worried about his brother told me the man had invested every penny he had in a business. The business went bankrupt and the man lost everything, including his mind. He had a nervous breakdown. He didn't recognize his wife and children; he forgot his own name.

I don't minimize the stress or pain this man experienced. Having Jesus in the center of your life doesn't mean you won't feel stress, failure, frustration, or helplessness.

It's more like the difference between two farms in Kansas. One was built with a storm cellar, the other without. When the first tornado hit, the farmer with the storm cellar went below and shut the door. After the tornado passed, both farms were utterly destroyed. But the farmer in the cellar was still there to rebuild. The other farmer was blown away with his house.

The other marks in the circle are in equally important positions. The spouse is near the center. Closer than the kids, the spouse should be second only to Jesus. This is so difficult because we fight against primal instincts. It doesn't mean you love your children less. If your relationship with your spouse is strong, your children learn lessons that affect the rest of their lives.

A common reason for divorce after long marriages (twenty or more years) is the empty nest syndrome. The parents have enveloped themselves with their children. While the children live at home, the couple relate to each other as Mommy and Daddy. They lose their spousal identity. Suddenly, the children are gone, the house is empty, and they have no idea what to talk about.

As one woman put it, "I lived for my children. My children left, and I didn't know who the man was who sat across the table from me. He looked familiar, but I couldn't think of his name. Not until the divorce papers came."

In remarriage, couples often get so caught up in fights

with the kids, the ex-spouse, and the finances, they forget why they married in the first place.

Without even realizing it, remarried couples change the structure of the circle. Problems begin to crowd into and toward the center of the sphere. Children fight for attention, and suddenly you can't find Jesus' dot, and your spouse has moved to the edge.

The reason you mark the problems outside the circle is a statement of perspective. As long as problems are kept on the peripheral of the family relationship, they pose little interference. The farmer who went into the storm cellar knew he belonged inside as long as the storm was outside. It was his place of refuge. Your home should be a place of refuge.

THE SECOND CIRCLE

In the first part of this chapter, you learned about the "ideal" circle of marriage. Now take a second piece of paper and draw another circle. It won't be as easy because you are the one who decides which dot goes where. This circle is the representation of your life right now; a picture of priorities. Draw the picture not as you would like it to be, but as you see it now.

When you have finished your new masterpiece, compare it to the first circle. What are the differences? If you are like many people, it is difficult to place the dots exactly. Some facets of our lives are always changing places of priority. But you should be able to pinpoint their positions most of the time.

Take a good look at the two pictures. Can you see how a poorly organized circle of priorities can ruin your marriage? Do you feel the roar of an approaching storm under your feet? Can you handle the tornado?

You need to be inside your circle with Jesus in the

middle and all the problems, on the peripheral.

How do you set your priorities in order?

JESUS FIRST

"Love the Lord your God with all your heart and with all your soul and with all your mind and with all your strength" (Mark 12:30).

Many people say Jesus is the center of their life. But if he does hold this position, where is proof of his residence? Too often a Christian is considered as a person who lives by a list of "doesn'ts." At work someone will say, "Yeah, he must be a Christian. He doesn't drink." Or maybe he does drink, but he doesn't smoke. Maybe he drinks and smokes, but he doesn't use profanity. Of course, he might drink, smoke, and swear, but he doesn't work on Sunday. Then again, he might be asleep all day on Sundays. . . .

Is that what your family sees? Others know when Jesus is in the center of your life. Consider this:

And we pray this in order that you may live a life worthy of the Lord and may please him in every way: *bearing fruit in every good work, growing in the knowledge of God, being strengthened with all power according to his glorious might so that you may have great endurance and patience, and joyfully giving thanks to the Father,* who has qualified you to share in the inheritance of the saints in the kingdom of light (Col. 1:10-12, italics added).

Not one "doesn't" appears in the whole passage.

SPOUSE SECOND

You can keep your spouse in the number two position,

ahead of bills, kids, and in-laws, by telling him where he stands. Often. When financial problems bang on your door, it is a balm of peace to say, "I know things seem pretty bad, but we'll get through. I'd rather be poor with you than rich without you."

Do you believe it? You do, deep down. If I had a medical degree on the wall, and I came to you and said, "Your husband/wife has two weeks to live," would money problems seem so terrible anymore? Would any of your present maladies be as important?

Such questions are not morbid. They're realistic. We waste our time and energy on stupid things. We fight over stupid things. I have attended two funerals where the deceased were openly eulogized for traits that irritated their spouses. Why must we appreciate what we don't have?

I asked a woman who had been married twenty-seven years how long it had been since she'd met her husband at the door with a kiss. She smiled shyly. "Twenty years."

I asked the husband how long it had been since he'd gone straight to his wife from the door just to give her a hug or kiss. He had to think a little harder. "Twenty-one or twenty-two years, I guess."

Is your spouse important to you?

CHILDREN AND PROBLEMS

Children and problems are lumped under the same heading because they are transient. They change constantly, and eventually, they go away. New problems always crop up, but practice makes them easier to handle.

The way children and problems affect your life is often dependent on your first two priorities. If Jesus is first, your spouse second, you have a solid foundation to brace yourself for kids and stress.

A child's safety comes before a spouse, as in cases of

abuse. But parent-child relationships are much less turbulent for the mother or father who does not make a child the center of life. The child in the number one or even number two spot is in control of the parent. This frightens the child, who lacks the maturity for such responsibility. It also frustrates the parent.

In the non-abusive family, there is no reason to put children before the spouse. If you do so, you lose. Your child loses. And you've lost your partner.

TIME TO CONSIDER

In every marriage, most problems can be traced to one source: misaligned priorities. When your priorities are out of order, you can work and work and work some more. But the result is the same.

I know you've worked hard. Is that sweat? Or are you crying?

1. Have you made Jesus first in your life? Could you prove it by the people who know you?

2. How do you know when Jesus is in the right position in your life? What are the results?

3. When was the last time you kissed or hugged your spouse in such a way that said, "I love you more than anything on earth"? I'm not talking about "Hi, dear, I'm home." Peck, peck. I mean the real thing.

4. Do you feel guilty if you put your spouse's wishes over your children's? Do you make it up to your children with an attitude of "Let's humor him/her"?

5. Your children are learning how to be married from you. What are they learning?

11

...

Negotiation, Nail-Biting, and Neurotics

Sounds seeped in through the cracks of Stranger's sleep. As they penetrated, his mind fought for the safety of unconscious refuge. But he could not resist the pull toward reality and finally he opened his eyes. Stranger turned his head to the side.

He had to blink to bring the room into focus, but as he did so, Stranger saw the old man on a chair at the table. Working. The room was as it had always been. Had he dreamed it all? Perhaps he had not seen the picture at all! But why was he so stiff?

The old man turned in his chair to look at Stranger. "Ah, you're awake. I'm glad."

Stranger cleared his throat. His mouth felt thick and sticky. Slowly, he raised himself to a sitting position. He looked out the window and could see it was still dark outside. How much time had passed?

The old man followed Stranger's gaze and said, "The sun will rise at the next hour."

Stranger made no reply. He continued to look about the room. Where did this bed come from? Finally, his eyes rested on the table. The picture was there as before. No, not as before. The puzzle appeared to be close to completion. How?

His head and chest felt heavy. Too heavy to hold up alone. He drew his legs to his chest, folded his arms on top of his knees, and rested his forehead upon his arms. "Why?" he asked.

The old man came to the bed and sat on the end. His voice was low and smooth. As he spoke, his words wrapped around Stranger like a blanket that soothed his battered body and soul. "Why didn't I tell you it was your picture, your life? You would have swept it away before I had a chance to work at all. Or you would have wanted instant results." He waited for a response from Stranger. There was none.

"Why your puzzle? Why did I dig out rubbish so painful to you that you threw it away? Because I love you. You are a part of this puzzle. If you throw it away, you throw yourself away. I want you. I want you whole."

Stranger made no movement or sound.

"I know what you ask. Why did I allow all this pain, all the bitter pieces in your puzzle? If I love you, why did you get hurt? I will tell you what I can for now, but you won't understand until your eyes have opened to the new sun. I have chosen you for brilliance. For color. For the promise in rainbows."

In the silence that echoed the old man's words, Stranger raised his head and looked into the ageless face. "Why would you choose me for this? I have been a stranger to

106

you. You are right. If I had known in the beginning it was my puzzle you worked on, I would have returned it to the pit you found it in. I threw it away because I couldn't stand it anymore. I couldn't stand the memories, and I hated the possibilities. But you, you know my life but not my name; you retrieved the bitterness of my heart and coerced me to help you bring it back to existence!" Stranger's accusation flew at the old man. But instead of defense or anger, which Stranger expected, the old man smiled.

"I know your name," he said, "for I have given it to you."

"Christians and people who love each other should never fight." The woman who said this to me had lived her beliefs. In twenty-two years of marriage, she had rarely spoken harsh words to her husband. She could not bring herself to verbally disagree with him. Had she attained an ideal marriage? No. For twenty-two years this couple lived in the same house, ate the same meals, and slept in the same bed. But they never touched.

Ignoring a problem does not resolve conflict. This woman's husband had a volatile temperament. With each explosion on his part, she built a wall of defense. She closed her mouth and did dishes. If her feelings were hurt, she cried in secret. When she was angry, she pushed it down inside.

Her husband never felt the need to apologize. If her feelings were hurt, she'd tell him—right?

This couple never learned to negotiate. With each conflict they grew farther apart. A successful marriage is not measured in the number of years you can stand to live together. It is measured in your ability to give and receive love and respect.

At a large gathering of my husband's relatives, I

witnessed an example of a successful marriage. Gordon's Aunt Rose and Uncle Wally. I had known them for years, even before I married Gordon, but on this day I noticed something special. Aunt Rose and Uncle Wally were in love. Every chance he could, Uncle Wally found Aunt Rose and gave her a bear hug. It didn't matter where she was or who she was talking to, Aunt Rose got hugged.

Months later, when I told Aunt Rose I'd spied on the two of them, she laughed. "The Lord knew I needed a hugger. I have gone through so much physical and emotional pain lately; I've taken a lot of it out on Wally. He just smiles and hugs me more. I can't help but hug him back."

Neither Aunt Rose or Uncle Wally are perfect people. They get irritable, temperamental, and hurt. But they have learned to negotiate in the tough times so the good times are great.

THE ART OF NEGOTIATION

Negotiation skills aren't inherited. They are learned. That's bad news for people who say, "That's just the way I am."

You can and must learn to *practice* negotiation techniques to have a successful marriage.

The definition of negotiate is pertinent when used in marital conflict. Webster defines negotiate like this: "To confer or bargain, one with another, in order to reach an agreement." Also: "To succeed in moving through, over, or around; as to *negotiate* a difficult place or situation."

Both definitions apply to our purpose. Marriage partners learn to bargain and confer with one another so they can move through, over, or around difficult situations in their relationships. This process of negotiation works best when applied by both partners but can still be used successfully by one person. By mastering negotiation skills, you learn to control confrontations.

Several key techniques are used in constructive negotiation. As you read the following list, commit them to memory and pray about them. And practice, practice, practice!

THE FINER POINTS

1) *Control your temper.* This may be the most important step in the art of negotiation. Anger is offensive and forces the other person to take a defensive position. Proverbs 30:33 provides graphic illustration of angry negotiations: "For as churning the milk produces butter, and as twisting the nose produces blood, so stirring up anger produces strife."

Think back to the last time you and your spouse were angry with each other. Accusations flew back and forth, sarcasm oozed. Later, you might have exchanged apologies and made up. Yet sharp words leave wounds. Wounds leave scars. You can say you're sorry for two days, but it won't erase the words you spoke in anger.

2) *Talk.* Have you ever tried to negotiate with someone who won't talk to you? It's incredibly frustrating. Silence is the murderer of marriage.

Penny and Jack fought in fits of silence. It was not uncommon for them to live in virtual silence for two or three weeks at a time. With every passing day, their hearts became harder and harder toward each other. After six years of tense quiet, they spoke calmly, rationally about divorce. In divorce, they accomplished what they could not in marriage. They talked.

3) *Listen.* Negotiation can almost be considered a game. Games have rules. Rules make the game more enjoyable because everyone has the same advantages and disadvantages. There should be at least one rule in negotiation. Listen when the other person speaks. Hear the words,

watch the face, and study the tone. Really listen.

James gives us excellent advice: "My dear brothers, [*sisters too*] take note of this: Everyone should be *quick to listen, slow to speak and slow to become angry*" (James 1:19 italics added).

This verse summarizes all that is involved in skillful negotiation. Two people who understand and follow this verse can work out any problem.

4) *Trade shoes.*

For this reason he had to be made like his brothers in every way, in order that he might become a merciful and faithful high priest in service to God, and that he might make atonement for the sins of the people. *Because he himself suffered when he was tempted, he is able to help those who are being tempted* (Heb. 2:17,18 italics added).

Jesus walked in our shoes. He is qualified to say, "I know how you feel." Our personal relationship with Jesus is based on his willingness to suffer. His suffering enabled him to understand how we think and feel.

Try to look at problems through your spouse's eyes. Strive to understand why certain acts or words hurt or irritate. It's easy to say, "How would *you* feel if I did that to you?" But turn it around. Can you say, "How would *I* feel if he/she did that to me?"

5) *Use constructive phrasing.* Read the following phrases, and choose the set you would respond to most positively:

A) "How come you never. . . ."

"I hate it when you. . . ."

"Just once, I wish you would. . . ."

B) "It makes me feel good when you. . . ."

"Please tell me when I do. . . ."

"I wish we could. . . ."

Successful negotiation depends on tact. If you can say something without insult or threat, say it. If you can't, zip the lips.

6) *Forget about pride and rights.* This is where most negotiations fail. Pride and rights. "Pride only breeds quarrels, but wisdom is found in those who take advice" (Prov. 13:10).

How many times have you heard, "I have a right to be mad!" Or better yet, how many times have you said it? I say it all the time. When I'm upset or hurt I tend to close up and boil. I think about everything I've done for people since I was six months old and how I get no appreciation. I say to myself, "I have a *right* to be angry!"

After a few years of righteous indignation and self pity, I learned something. I may have the right, but what good does it do me? If I can't even touch my husband because of my righteous anger, who is being punished? Who is the loser? When I give up my right to anger and swallow my pride, I realize I may be one of the most blessed women alive. I have a pretty nice husband. I almost let my pride and rights ruin that.

7) *Let yourself laugh.* You've tried the above six steps and you still aren't talking. It's time to laugh. Quit taking yourself so seriously.

I don't get mad often, but when I do I'm either terrifying or comical. It depends on your sense of humor. I married a man with a sense of humor.

When Gordon and I were newlyweds, he wore a full beard. It was perfect. Perfect temptation. We were in an argument one night about something extremely important. It was probably about goldfish or something equally life-and-death. I reached the point of eruption and started a verbal tirade that knocked pine cones from the trees outside. I was mad. As I assaulted him with my words, all I could think about was, "Man! I want to pull that beard!"

I got closer and closer to him, shaking my extended finger in his face, trying to resist the temptation to grab and yank.

In the middle of my "*If you ever . . . ,*" Gordon laughed. My finger stopped an inch from his nose. My lower jaw dropped, and I couldn't say a word. Gordon laughed harder. In fact, my tall, rugged husband laughed so hard he cried.

Finally, he chuckled out, "I wish you could've seen yourself! Waving that finger under my nose . . ." and he went on laughing. I laughed, too, because I *could* see myself in a mirror. I looked pretty ridiculous. I also told Gordon how close I came to pulling his beard. I've always wondered why he shaved it off that week.

TIME TO CONSIDER

Why should you work so hard to make your marriage last? Why should you try when your partner has already given up or doesn't seem to care? Don't do it for your husband or wife. Work for the Lord.

Whatever you do, work at it with all your heart, as working for the Lord, not for men, since you know that you will receive an inheritance from the Lord as a reward. *It is the Lord Christ you are serving* (Col. 3:23,24 italics added).

1. How do you and your spouse communicate during disagreements? Cold silence? Through microphones and amplifiers? Through the mail?

2. How would you like to communicate?

3. What grudges are stored away in your memory banks? How and why should you get rid of them?

4. Jesus is the Son of God. He is higher than the angels. What rights were his according to his royal birth? What rights did he demand while he lived on earth?

Now some homework. The next time you are angry, ask yourself three questions:

1. I have a right to be angry. But will my anger change the other person or his/her actions?

2. I have a right to be angry. But does it make me feel better?

3. I have a right to be angry. What have I accomplished?

12

· · ·

To Toss or to Preserve, that Is the Question

The old man continued to speak as he went back to the table. "I know your name because I named you. I knew you in your mother's womb." He began to place the few remaining pieces into the puzzle. "I saw your birth and observed your growth. I watched you make mistakes. I tried to warn you at times, but you didn't hear me. Once you heard me. You heard my words, but you followed your own desires. You are a stranger only to yourself for I have loved you unconditionally, always." The last piece of the puzzle fell in to rest among the conglomeration of Stranger's life.

Stranger's anger could not stand against the onslaught of such great love. He felt the hurt, the bitterness, dissolve and fade. But pain and pity had filled his heart for so long it now felt void. It was empty. "What name have you given me?"

"You are Benaiah. It is Hebrew, and it means: 'Yahweh has built up.' What you destroyed, I have built up."

"Benaiah." Stranger let the name permeate his sodden heart. "I am no longer a stranger. My name is Benaiah." He rose and approached the table. "It's finished. You finished the picture."

The old man shook his head. "No, Benaiah. I put the puzzle back together, but you must finish it. As it is now, it will fall apart when the wind blows, or," he added with a spark of humor, "if the table should tip. I leave this final decision to you, Benaiah. Do you finish the puzzle or not?"

Benaiah saw no other pieces, no work to be done. But he knew what the old man said was true. The picture he beheld was fragile. The startling colors and the quite visible gaps would never hold together on their own. "What can I do? How do I make it complete?"

The old man crossed the room to a dusty shelf. At the back of the shelf was a clay jar. He reached up and pulled down the jar, then returned to the table. Holding the jar at arms length, the old man handed it to Benaiah. "Take it. It is the sweet blood of my own son. He shed his blood for this purpose. If you want the puzzle preserved, the blood must be poured over it. It is a choice only you can make."

Pour blood on the picture! How could blood hold together his discarded life? Benaiah looked at the old man. He looked at the picture and made his decision. He let the blood spill out onto the puzzle. The stream of red formed rivulets that sought out cracks, crevices, and gaps. When the jar was empty, no slit could be found between any of the puzzle pieces. The jumbled collage was filled and cemented by precious fluid.

"There is one thing more to be done." The old man picked up the picture and walked to the window. He raised *the colored confusion until the bottom of the picture reached the sill. Gently he pushed and the shades of dawn were held back. The picture filled the square window perfectly.*

"Watch now, Benaiah. You will see my purpose. You will understand my plan."

Benaiah watched. His heart thumped solid thuds against his chest. He tasted anticipation as it sat upon his tongue. A burst of brilliance splashed against the back of the picture as dawn broke. The puzzle could not subdue the light of the Son, and it was transformed from chaotic bits and pieces into order and beauty. Paper and cardboard became stained glass and precious stones held firm by sacrifice. The picture, once fractured and hopeless, was now sacred and whole.

One of the most beautiful stories I heard during the hundred plus interviews with remarried couples was told to me by someone I'll name Shannon. Shannon hadn't been married before, but it was her husband Larry's second marriage. Many of their problems were repercussions of Larry's first marriage. Repressed hurt and anger prevented Larry from fully trusting Shannon and stinted his ability to talk about problems. After two years of fighting a ghost, Shannon said, "It isn't worth it. I'm leaving."

She picked up the telephone, dialed her parent's number, and sobbed, "Dad, can you pick me up? I'm leaving Larry. I can't stand it anymore. Please come and get me."

After her father agreed to help her move home, Shannon walked into her bedroom and waited. Larry sat alone in the living room. Within a few minutes, the doorbell rang, and Larry answered it. He opened the door to face his father-in-law.

In a quiet but firm voice, Shannon's father said, "I came

here to pick up my daughter and take her home. As a father, I love her and want to take her with me. As a Christian, I know I can't do that. So I'm going to stay here with you until we get all this straightened out. I won't leave until we do." He walked past Larry, sat on the couch, and folded his arms.

As Shannon finished telling me this story, she said, "That was the beginning of our marriage. I couldn't leave, and Larry was forced to talk to me. He was angry at first, but we worked things out. It was a good thing, too, because my father wouldn't leave until we did. The Lord used my dad to save my marriage."

Remember the dirty fingers in the salad bowl? Shannon's father made a choice. The easiest thing for a father to do would be to get his fingers dirty; commiserate and whisk his daughter away from her unhappiness. Instead, he made her face her problems. His presence assured her of his love, but he would not help her run away. And Larry responded to the obvious caring his father-in-law displayed.

Another facet in this story is the crisis itself. Shannon came to a point in her marriage when it seemed useless to continue. She was bereft of energy and desolate of spirit. It was over. Hopeless. All that was left to hold the couple together was a father who wanted to do God's will.

It was enough. Shannon and Larry have now been married for twelve years. Is this a marriage made in heaven? No. It is made on earth out of rocks and hard places. But it's also filled with meadows and mountains, oceans and birds.

Every marriage has at least a thin thread of hope. It may not even be in you or your spouse. In this case, the father is the only one who had any hope. Hope doesn't make a marriage, but it is a reason to try.

WHERE DO WE GO FROM HERE?

I am not in your shoes. It is not my right, responsibility, or desire to tell you what to do. Of one thing I am certain: if you are reading this book because you're remarried and having problems, hope is inside of you. You haven't completely given up. Hang on to your hope.

A Christian's marriage certificate does not come packaged with remote control. There's no promise in the Bible that says, "If you do what is right in the eyes of the Lord, so will everyone else." In fact, story after story illustrates the opposite. 2 Samuel 14 begins the story of King David and his son Absalom. Absalom had killed his brother and fled to hide from his father. But David loved Absalom and longed to see him.

Joab was David's friend. He knew David's sorrow and conspired to bring Absalom back to Jerusalem. David allowed Absalom to return but would not permit Absalom to look upon his face. For two years, Absalom lived in the city without seeing his father. Joab begged to intervene once more, and David relented.

For the next four years, while exhibiting love and devotion for his father, Absalom plotted. He gathered troops and turned the people of Israel against David. Finally, he sent messengers out to proclaim himself as king of Israel. David was forced to flee for his life. Barefoot, he climbed the Mount of Olives, weeping as he went.

Did David weep for the loss of his kingdom? No. David wept as a father for a child. David had done everything possible for the son he loved. He forgave him of murder. He shared with him materially. When Absalom first returned to David's court, Absalom laid face down in submission to the king; David lifted him up and kissed him. David loved Absalom. Absalom tried to steal his father's kingdom, sleep with his concubines, and order his death.

Was David at fault for Absalom's actions? Could David control Absalom's behavior or decisions by his own righteous acts?

David's story is your story. Like David, you have a responsibility to do what God wants you to do. But you can't control Absalom.

GOD'S EXPECTATIONS

I agonize over difficult decisions. When I pray, I say, "Lord, what do you want me to do? Hit me with a brick or something! Make it obvious so even I can understand."

Such a prayer is an invitation for pain. I've got bumps all over my head where I've been struck by flying bricks. Of course, that doesn't mean I always did what God wanted.

A lot of bricks are in the Bible. God's expectations for you and for your marriage are in writing.

Let us therefore make every effort to do what leads to peace and to mutual edification (Rom. 14:19).

The husband should fulfill his marital duty to his wife, and likewise the wife to her husband. The wife's body does not belong to her alone but also to her husband. In the same way, the husband's body does not belong to him alone but also to his wife (1 Cor. 7:3,4).

Flee the evil desires of youth, and pursue righteousness, faith, love and peace, along with those who call on the Lord out of a pure heart. Don't have anything to do with foolish and stupid arguments, because you know they produce quarrels (2 Tim. 2:22,23).

Be patient, then, brothers, until the Lord's coming.

See how the farmer waits for the land to yield its valuable crop and how patient he is for the fall and spring rains. You too, be patient and stand firm, because the Lord's coming is near (James 5:7,8).

Haven't you read, he replied, that at the beginning the Creator "made them male and female," and said, "For this reason a man will leave his father and mother and be united to his wife, and the two will become one flesh"? So they are no longer two, but one. Therefore what God has joined together, let man not separate (Matt. 19:4-6).

CAN MY MARRIAGE BE SAVED?

Remember ideals? Ideally, yes, your marriage *can* be saved. Even abusive situations have been changed by God. In such cases, drastic measures were taken, such as removing the victims from the home, and intense counseling took place. But God has healed many abusive marriages.

God loves the impossible. Jesus excels in the impossible. But in every miracle Jesus performed, he required one thing of the recipient. A step of faith. In some cases, the step was literal.

Jesus healed a certain paralytic. His first words to the man were, "Take heart, son; your sins are forgiven."

The man didn't jump up off his mat at these words. He waited while Jesus debated with a few teachers who accused him of blasphemy. Jesus then told the paralytic, " *'Get up, take your mat and go home.'* And the man got up and went home" (Matt. 9:2-6 italics added).

Why didn't the man jump up when Jesus forgave his sins?

In another town, a synagogue ruler named Jairus came and fell at Jesus' feet. His words to Jesus are the expression of every parent's fear, "My little daughter is dying. Please come and put your hands on her so that she will be healed and live."

Before Jesus reached the man's home, a messenger came to Jairus. "Your daughter is dead," he said. "Why bother the teacher any more?" (I would refer this messenger back to chapter eleven to read about tact.)

Ignoring the messenger, Jesus told the synagogue ruler, "Don't be afraid; just believe." He went into the house and said to the body of the little girl, *"Talitha koum!"* or "Little girl, I say to you, get up!" The girl stood up (see Mark 5:21-42).

On the way to Jairus' house, a woman touched Jesus' cloak and was healed. He felt the power go out from him and asked who touched him. The woman admitted touching his hem to receive healing. Jesus said, "Daughter, your faith has healed you. Go in peace and be freed from your suffering" (Mark 5:34).

What does Jesus say to you about your marriage? Two things. "Don't be afraid; just believe" and "Get up, get going! Do something!"

Would the paralytic have been healed if he refused to stand up? Would the girl have lived if her father had given up when the messenger came? The woman was not healed at the sight of Jesus. She touched his clothes. It was a combination of faith and action.

IN THE MEANTIME

Many people whom Jesus healed endured a waiting period. Mary and Martha waited several days for Jesus, and Lazarus died. Jairus' daughter also died before Jesus could get to his house. It's hard to wait for the Lord. We want help now. Can you make it on your own until he comes?

Four months after my third child was born, I participated

in a triathalon. If you aren't familiar with triathalons, they are a combination of three sporting events. This particular triathalon consisted of a half-mile swim in a lake, an eighteen-mile bike ride, and a four-and-a-half-mile run. You get on a bicycle as you get out of the water, you run (or in my case, wobble) when you get off the bike.

Five hundred people jumped into the lake when the start gun barked. Three hundred ninety-five finished.

I did okay in the swim. I wasn't first, but I left a few in the water. The bicycle stage was harder. My legs were chafed, and I thought I would never reach the school where the run began. I kept thinking, "If I can reach the school, I can finish the race. I just have to get off this bike."

At last, I reached the school. Someone held my bike and helped lift my leg over the bar so I could get off. Now to run.

My legs forgot how. My feet went in different directions.

In a drunken forward motion, I moved. Sort of. People constantly ran past me. Runners are born encouragers. They clapped for me as they went by and yelled, "Come on! You can do it! Keep going!" Then they disappeared over the next hill.

I ran alone. I hurt. I was lonely. I was embarrassed. At regular intervals along the run, tables were set up with hundreds of cups of orange juice. By the time I reached the first juice stop, there was one cup on the table. Several volunteers standing by a van saw me approach and yelled and clapped. "Come on, you can do it!" They thrust the juice into my hand as I hobbled by.

The same truck with the same people were at the next station. "Come on! You can do it!" they cried when they saw me coming.

The same thing happened at each refreshment center until finally I had less than a mile to go. I watched my feet take each blistered step-jog. One more step. One more step. Then I heard my name. I looked up and saw my sister Cindy running toward me. She had finished the race half an hour before. As she reached me, she turned around and began to jog with me at my stuttered pace.

"I came to finish the race with you," she said.

I couldn't talk. I needed to breathe.

One hour past eternity, we reached the school. The race finished on the oval track in front of a small group of bleachers. To my amazement, there were still people in the bleachers. I was twenty minutes behind the last runner, and they had waited for me. As Cindy and I entered the oval, the small crowd cheered like crazy. My legs worked harder, and I was able to semi-sprint around the oval to the finish line. I could hear the people cheering, "You can do it!"

It didn't matter to the people who waited for me that I finished last in the race. What mattered to them, my sister, my husband, and to me was that I finished the race. Every time I heard, "Come on! You can do it!" my feet carried me a few more steps. I tried harder.

You are in the toughest race of your life. You hurt, your feet are blistered. How can you go on? The writer of Hebrews says,

> Therefore, since we are surrounded by such a great cloud of witnesses, let us throw off everything that hinders and the sin that so easily entangles, and let us run with perseverance the race marked out for us. Let us fix our eyes on Jesus, the author and perfecter of our faith, who for the joy set before him endured the cross, scorning its shame, and sat down at the right hand of the throne of God (Heb. 12:1,2).

With every impossible step you take to repair your marriage, a great cloud of witnesses is cheering you on. They are people who understand impossible odds. People like Noah, Moses, Gideon, David, and Esther. They ran on ahead of you, and now they sit in the bleachers and yell, "Come on! You can do it!"

Now you are less than a mile away. Listen. It's your name. Jesus came back to finish the race with you. You aren't alone anymore.

God wants your marriage to be a glorious testament to his power over impossible situations. He wants you to finish your race, not staggering; sprinting.

TIME TO CONSIDER

Complete your puzzle. He'll help you. He'll reshape the pieces and make them fit. Everything you thought was useless he will use to create a new picture.

Are you like Benaiah, ready to sweep the puzzle away before it is finished? Are you angry because it takes so long to finish? Wait with God. Every piece will find its place in your life. Then when the puzzle is complete, accept the clay jar, and pour Christ's blood over the picture. Let him fill in the cracks and crevices. Set the whole jumbled mess in front of the Light, and watch the transformation.

"Come on! You can do it!"

1. God says to you, "Get up. Go." What do you think he wants you to do in your marriage?

2. Look back over the last year. What changes have occured that one year and one day ago you thought were impossible to change?

3. What is the most impossible situation you face in

your marriage right now? How would you like God to change it?

4. Your situation may not change, or it may get worse. How would that affect your faith and relationship with Jesus?

5. How can God change you for the better? How would these changes affect your marital relationship?

6. Do you have people who cheer for you? Who are they? How do they make you feel?

7. You've finished the book. What will you do now?

Dear Jesus,

My prayer for the people who read this book is simple. May they feel love, hope, and peace. Help them to know I am cheering for them; and there are others waiting in the bleachers. Most of all, may they see your glory in impossibilities.

Amen.

Source Notes

Chapter Two

1. *The New Book of American Ratings,* (New York: FYI Information Services, 1982), p. 51.
2. *International Encyclopedia of Population,* Vol. 2, (The Free Press, 1982), p. 175.
3. Visher and Visher, *Step Families: A Guide to Working With Stepparents and Stepchildren,* (Larchmont, NY: Bruner/Mazel, 1979).

Chapter Three

1. Tom and Adrienne Frydenger, *The Blended Family,* (Grand Rapids, MI: Chosen Books, 1985), p. 40.

Chapter Four

1. Glynnis Walker, *Second Wife, Second Best?* (New York, NY: Doubleday and Co., 1984), p. 14.
2. Jamie K. Keshet, *Love and Power in the Stepfamily: A Practical Guide,* (Scarborough, Ontario, Canada: McGraw-Hill, 1987), p. 161.

Chapter Nine

1. Dr. Chuck James, personal interview. Sumner, WA, February 19, 1989.
2. Ibid.

Support Group Leader's Guide

Issue-oriented, problem-wrestling, life-confronting—Heart Issue books are appropriate for adult Sunday school classes, individual study, and especially for support groups. Here are guidelines to encourage and facilitate support groups.

SUPPORT GROUP GUIDELINES

The small group setting offers individuals the opportunity to commit themselves to personal growth through mutual caring and support. This is especially true of Christian support groups, where from five to twelve individuals meet on a regular basis with a mature leader to share their personal experiences and struggles over a specific "heart issue." In such a group, individuals develop trust and accountability with each other and the Lord. Because a support group's purpose differs from a Bible study or prayer group, it needs its own format and guidelines.

Let's look at the ingredients of a support group:

- Purpose
- Leadership
- Meeting Format
- Group Guidelines

PURPOSE

The purpose of a Heart Issue support group is to provide:

1. An *opportunity* for participants to share openly and honestly their struggles and pain over a specific issue in a non-judgmental, Christ-centered framework.

2. A *"safe place"* where participants can gain perspective on a mutual problem and begin taking responsibility for their responses to their own situations.

3. An *atmosphere* that is compassionate, understanding, and committed to challenging participants from a biblical perspective.

Support groups are not counseling groups. Participants come to be supported, not fixed or changed. Yet, as genuine love and caring are exchanged, people begin to experience God's love and acceptance. As a result, change and healing take place.

The initiators of a support group need to be clear about its specific purpose. The following questions are examples of what to consider before starting a small group.

1. What type of group will this be? A personal growth group, a self-help group, or a group structured to focus on a certain theme? Is it long-term, short-term, or ongoing?

2. Who is the group for? A particular population? College students? Single women? Divorced people?

3. What are the goals for the group? What will members gain from it?

4. Who will lead or co-lead the group? What are his/her qualifications?

5. How many members should be in the group? Will new members be able to join the group once it is started?

6. What kind of structure or format will the group have?

7. What topics will be explored in the support book and to what degree will this be determined by the group members and to what degree by the leaders?

LEADERSHIP

Small group studies often rotate leadership among participants, but because support groups usually meet for a specific time period with a specific mutual issue, it works well to have one leader or a team of co-leaders responsible for the meetings.

Good leadership is essential for a healthy, balanced group. Qualifications include character and personality traits as well as life experience and, in some cases, professional experience.

Personal Leadership Characteristics

COURAGE

One of the most important traits of effective group leaders is courage. Courage is shown in willingness (1) to be open to self-disclosure, admitting their own mistakes and taking the same risks they expect others to take; (2) to confront another, and, in confronting, to understand that love is the goal; (3) to act on their beliefs and hunches; (4) to be emotionally touched by another and to draw on their experiences in order to identify with the other; (5) to continually examine their inner self; (6) to be direct and honest with members; and (7) to express to the group their fears and expectations about the group process. (Leaders shouldn't use their role to protect themselves from honest and direct interaction with the rest of the group.)

WILLINGNESS TO MODEL

Through their behavior, and the attitudes conveyed by it, leaders can create a climate of openness, seriousness of purpose, acceptance of others, and the desirability of taking risks. Group leaders should have had some moderate victory in their own struggles, with adequate healing having taken place. They recognize their own woundedness and see themselves as persons in process as well. Group leaders lead largely by example—by doing what they expect members to do.

PRESENCE

Group leaders need to be emotionally present with the group members. This means being touched by others' pain, struggles, and joys. Leaders can become more emotionally involved with others by paying close attention to their own reactions and by permitting these reactions to become intense. Fully experiencing emotions gives leaders the ability to be compassionate and empathetic with their members. At the same time, group leaders understand their role as facilitators. They know they're not answer people; they don't take responsibility for change in others.

GOODWILL AND CARING

A sincere interest in the welfare of the others is essential in group leaders. Caring involves respecting, trusting, and valuing people. Not every member is easy to care for, but leaders should at least want to care. It is vital that leaders become aware of the kinds of people they care for easily and the kinds they find it difficult to care for. They can gain this awareness by openly exploring their reactions to members. Genuine caring must be demonstrated; merely saying so is not enough.

Some ways to express a caring attitude are: (1) inviting a person to participate but allowing that person to decide how far to go; (2) giving warmth, concern, and support when, and only when it is genuinely felt; (3) gently confronting the person when there are obvious discrepancies between a person's words and her behavior; and (4) encouraging people to be what they could be without their masks and shields. This kind of caring requires a commitment to love and a sensitivity to the Holy Spirit.

OPENNESS

To be effective, group leaders must be open with themselves, open to others in groups, open to new experiences, and open to life-styles and values that differ from their own. Openness is an attitude. It doesn't mean that leaders reveal every aspect of their personal lives; it means that they reveal enough of themselves to give the participants a sense of person.

Leader openness tends to foster a spirit of openness within the group; it permits members to become more open about their feelings and beliefs; and it lends a certain fluidity to the group process. Self-revelation should not be manipulated as a technique. However, self-evaluation is best done spontaneously, when appropriate.

NONDEFENSIVENESS

Dealing frankly with criticism is related closely to openness. If group leaders are easily threatened, insecure in their work of leading, overly sensitive to negative feedback, and depend highly on group approval, they will probably encounter major problems in trying to carry out their leadership role. Members sometimes accuse leaders of not caring enough, of being selective in their caring, of structuring the sessions too much, of not providing enough direction, of being too harsh. Some criticism may be fair, some unfair. The crucial thing for leaders is to nondefensively explore with their groups the feelings that are legitimately produced by the leaders and those that represent what is upsetting the member.

STRONG SENSE OF SELF

A strong sense of self (or personal power) is an important quality of leaders. This doesn't mean that leaders would manipulate or dominate; it means that leaders are confident of who they are and what they are about. Groups "catch" this and feel the leaders know what they are doing. Leaders who have a strong sense of self recognize their weaknesses and don't expend energy concealing them from others. Their vulnerability becomes their strength as leaders. Such leaders can accept credit where it's due, and at the same time encourage members to accept credit for their own growth.

STAMINA

Group leading can be taxing and draining as well as exciting and energizing. Leaders need physical and emotional stamina and the ability to withstand pressure in order to remain vitalized until the group sessions end. If leaders give in to fatigue when the group bogs down, becomes resistive, or when members drop out, the effectiveness of the whole group could suffer. Leaders must be aware of their own energy level, have outside sources of spiritual and emotional nourishment, and have realistic expectations for the group's progress.

SENSE OF HUMOR

The leaders who enjoy humor and can incorporate it appropriately into the group will bring a valuable asset to the meetings. Sometimes humor surfaces as an escape from healthy confrontations and sensitive leaders need to identify and help the group avoid this diversion. But because we often take ourselves and our problems so seriously, we need the release of humor to bring balance and perspective. This is particularly true after sustained periods of dealing seriously with intensive problems.

CREATIVITY

The capacity to be spontaneously creative, to approach each group session with fresh ideas is a most important characteristic for group leaders. Leaders who are good at discovering new ways of approaching a group and who are willing to suspend the use of established techniques are unlikely to grow stale. Working with interesting co-leaders is another way for leaders to acquire fresh ideas.

GROUP LEADERSHIP SKILLS

Although personality characteristics of the group leader are extremely significant, by themselves they do not insure a healthy group. Leadership skills are also essential. The following need to be expressed in a sensitive and timely way:

ACTIVE LISTENING

Leaders need to absorb content, note gestures, observe subtle changes in voice or expression, and sense underlying messages. For example, a woman may be talking about her warm and loving feelings toward her husband, yet her body may be rigid and her fists clenched.

EMPATHY

This requires sensing the subjective world of the participant. Group leaders, in addition to being caring and open, must learn to grasp another's experience and at the same time maintain their separateness.

RESPECT AND POSITIVE REGARD

In giving support, leaders need to draw on the positive assets of the members. Where differences occur, there needs to be open and honest appreciation and toleration.

WARMTH

Smiling has been shown to be especially important in the communication of warmth. Other nonverbal means are: voice tone, posture, body language, and facial expression.

GENUINENESS

Leaders need to be real, to be themselves in relating with others, to be authentic and spontaneous.

FORMAT

The format of meetings will differ vastly from group to group, but the following are generally accepted as working well with support groups.

MEETING PLACE

This should be a comfortable, warm atmosphere. Participants need to feel welcome and that they've come to a "safe place" where they won't be overheard or easily distracted. Some groups will want to provide baby-sitting.

OPENING

Welcome participants. The leader should introduce herself and the members should also introduce themselves. It is wise to go over the "ground rules" at every meeting and especially at first or when there are newcomers. Some of these would include:

1. Respect others' sharing by keeping what is said in the group confidential.

2. Never belittle the beliefs or expressions of another.

3. Respect the time schedule. Try to arrive on time and be prompt in leaving.

4. Feel free to contact the leader at another time if there are questions or need for additional help.

Many meetings open with a brief time of prayer and worship and conclude with prayer. It often helps to ask for informal prayer requests and brief sharing so that the group begins in a spirit of openness.

MEETING

Leaders can initiate the meeting by focusing on a particular issue (or chapter if the group is studying a book). It is wise to define the focus of the specific meeting so that the group can stay on track for the entire session. (See Group Guidelines below.)

CLOSING

Strive for promptness without being abrupt. Give opportunity for those who need additional help to make an appointment with the leader. Be alert to any needing special affirmation or encouragement as they leave.

GROUP GUIDELINES

Because this is a support group, not an advice group, the leader will need to establish the atmosphere and show by her style how to relate lovingly and helpfully within the group. Participants need to know the guidelines for being a member of the group. It is a wise practice to repeat these guidelines at each meeting and especially when newcomers attend. The following guidelines have proven to be helpful to share with support groups:

1. You have come to give and receive support. No "fixing." We are to listen, support, and be supported by one another—not give advice.

2. Let other members talk. Please let them finish without interruption.

3. Try to step over any fear of sharing in the group. Yet do not monopolize the group's time.

4. Be interested in what someone else is sharing. Listen with your heart. Never converse privately with someone else while another member is addressing the group.

5. Be committed to express your feelings from the heart. Encourage others to do the same. It's all right to feel angry, to laugh, or to cry.

6. Help others own their feelings and take responsibility for change in their lives. Don't jump in with an easy answer or a story on how you conquered their problem. Relate to where they are.

7. Avoid accusing or blaming. Speak in the "I" mode about how something or someone made *you* feel. Example: "I felt angry when. . . ."

8. Avoid ill-timed humor to lighten emotionally charged times. Let participants work through their sharing even if it is hard.

9. Keep names and sharing of other group members confidential.

10. Because we are all in various stages of growth, please give newcomers permission to be new and old-timers permission to be further along in their growth. This is a "safe place" for all to grow and share their lives.